F HANDED

Souvik Bhadra earned his law degree from the National University of Juridical Sciences, Kolkata. He started his legal career with one of the major law firms of India and then worked as a partner at another law firm. Currently, Souvik divides his time between the Mumbai and Kolkata offices of Ashlar Law, a firm he has co-founded. He can be contacted at souvik.bhadra@gmail.com.

Pingal Khan also earned his law degree from the National University of Juridical Sciences, Kolkata. After graduation, Pingal co-founded a full service national law firm. Subsequently, Pingal co-founded Ashlar Law with Souvik and is currently based in Bangalore. He can be reached at pingalkhan@gmail.com.

RED

RED HANDED

20 Criminal Cases That Shook India

Souvik Bhadra • Pingal Khan

RUPA

Published by
Rupa Publications India Pvt. Ltd 2014
7/16, Ansari Road, Daryaganj
New Delhi 110002

Sales Centres:

Allahabad Bengaluru Chennai
Hyderabad Jaipur Kathmandu
Kolkata Mumbai

ISBN: 978-81-291-3481-3

Second impression 2016

10 9 8 7 6 5 4 3 2

The moral right of the authors has been asserted.

Printed by Replika Press Pvt. Ltd, Haryana

*We dedicate this book to the
late Professor Durgadas Banerjea,
for making criminal law easy, interesting and fun to learn.*

*We also dedicate the book to
our respective parents for being who they are.*

Contents

INTRODUCTION

'Criminals do not die by the hands of the law. They die by the hands of other men.'

—George Bernard Shaw

IT HAS BEEN said that society prepares the crime and the criminal commits it. A criminal is born not only when a person commits an offence written down in the statute books, but also, and more importantly, because his offence is deemed a crime by the world at large. The gravity of an offence or a crime is not determined only by the amount of punishment prescribed by the law, but also by the perception of the act as a crime in the eyes of society. For example, the practice of 'sati' continued in India for centuries in spite of it being an inhuman and deplorable act, since it was not seen as a 'crime' as per the standards of society at the time. Even the abolition of 'sati' and criminalizing it did not immediately end the practice because society still condoned it for years.

On the other hand, if a person is merely accused of committing a crime, or if strong suspicion is cast upon him, it is enough to create a strong enough impression on society to brand the individual as a criminal for life. During the British rule, ethnic and social communities in India which were defined as habitually criminal were systematically registered by the government. Restrictions on their movements were also imposed and adult male members of such groups were forced to report weekly to the local police. These 'criminal tribes' were de-notified after India gained independence. However, branding them as criminal tribes for over a century has led to discrimination and stereotyping even today, by society, the police and the media.

The role played by the media in the criminal justice scenario in India cannot be ignored. In the past few decades, extraneous circumstances have begun affecting decision-making in a criminal trial. The reactions of society to major crimes being committed within India is, of late, being moulded by the media to a great extent. Whenever a major crime like a murder or a rape takes place, within moments, the entire story is played out (and often dramatized) across news channels and is splashed all over the next day's newspapers. In India, trial by media, i.e., the declaration of innocence or guilt of the accused by television news and newspapers before or after a verdict in a court of law, has assumed much significance. As a majority of the Indian population is largely dependent on it for information, the influence that the media has on people is considerable. During high-profile court cases, the media is often accused of provoking an atmosphere of public hysteria that not only renders a fair trial nearly impossible, but also ensures that, regardless of the trial's result, the accused will have to live the rest of their lives under intense public scrutiny. On the other hand, it may be argued that the opinions of the public are formed independently and that the media merely voices them.

The media finds its defence under Article 19(1)(a) of the Constitution of India, which protects the fundamental right to freedom of speech, which has the right to know inherent in it. However, the central government is considering the Law Commission's 200th report, titled 'Trial by Media', which recommends an amendment to contempt of court laws, empowering the judiciary to impose restrictions on media reporting so as to curb possible interference in the administration of justice, protect fair trial and ensure the rights of the accused. The former Attorney General of India, late G.E. Vahanvati, had mentioned on 28 March 2012[1] that the government was actively considering these recommendations and seeking response from the state governments for preparing a draft law on the issue.

The Law Commission, when headed by Justice M. Jagannadha Rao back in 2006, had spoken of a need to empower the courts to pass 'postponement' orders to regulate publication. Meanwhile, though courts have held that the conditions for passing such orders of prior restraint should be allowed only under special circumstances, it is, however, accepted by the Supreme Court of India[2] time and again that temporary postponement of publication can be passed. This is, in fact, a norm in several jurisdictions around the globe, such as the United Kingdom, Australia, etc. It was added that publication of material prejudicial to the person after his arrest relating to his character, prior convictions and alleged confessions would also result in contempt of court. The justification given by the government of India was that the right to freedom of speech is for the benefit of the public and not the media.

---

[1]Dhananjay Mahapatra, 'Mulling law to curb trial by media, govt. tells SC', *Times of India* (New Delhi, 29 March 2012).

[2]Sahara India Real Estate Corp. Ltd & Ors. v. Securities and Exchange Board of India & Anr. (2012) 8 SCALE 101.

Trial by media in India has had a significant positive influence in seeking justice in several instances as well. Some famous criminal cases where the accused who were ultimately convicted would have otherwise gone unpunished had it not been for the intervention of the media are the Priyadarshini Mattoo case, the Jessica Lal case and the Nitish Katara murder case.

In the Jessica Lal case, for instance, the acquittal of the accused by the trial judge due to insufficient evidence and witnesses turning hostile led to public outcry. Both the national and international media highlighted this case as an instance of the skewed judicial process in India, which is often unduly influenced by the rich and powerful. As the public movement gathered momentum, the Delhi police approached the High Court to review of the case. This activism also helped shed light on an older case—that of Priyadarshini Mattoo—which had also been pending in the High Court. Human rights activists and the media took up the cause of that case too, and in light of this attention, the Delhi High Court took an unprecedented step and conducted a day-to-day hearing of the case and delivered its judgment in little over a month, convicting the accused.

As said above, the media plays an important role in shaping public opinion. Hence, the precautions that the government and the courts are trying to implement are not with the intention of restricting or curbing the freedom of the press, but rather to enhance its credibility and ensure that justice is meted out by those qualified to do so. It must be borne in mind that, in reality, the procedures followed by the criminal justice system are not represented in their entirety in the media.

Before examining the cases in this book, it would be useful to have a basic understanding of how the criminal justice system evolved in India and the structure of this system as it stands today.

THE CRIMINAL JUSTICE SYSTEM IN INDIA

The relationship between crime, society and the criminal justice system is as old as civilization. The system defines how a crime is investigated, evidence is gathered and arrests made. It is directed towards maintaining social order and welfare, preventing crime, punishing and rehabilitating the offenders and criminals, and to some extent, compensating the victims. This system in India consists of two main components: the law enforcement machinery and the judiciary. The task of the law enforcement machinery is to record and document reports of crime, investigate, gather evidence, arrest the offender and carry out any follow-up investigations as required.

The criminal justice system in India has evolved over centuries, starting from the Vedic age through the Islamic and Mughal periods and was finally formalized and codified in its present form under the British. Far-reaching changes were brought about by the British, including reorganizing the court system, organizing the police and drafting the Indian Penal Code (IPC), which is still in force today, albeit with some minor amendments. Our country follows the adversarial system, which means there are two sides to every case and each side presents its arguments to a neutral judge who then passes an order or a judgment based upon the merits of the case.

The Indian Penal Code is the principal criminal code of India intended to cover all the substantive aspects of criminal law. Under this comprehensive code, every person found guilty of committing an act contrary to the provisions stated in the code is punished, either with fine or imprisonment or, 'in rarest of rare' cases[3], death. The Code of Criminal Procedure (CrPC) is the procedural law which provides the machinery for punishment of offenders. It lists a very elaborate procedure which is to be followed during investigation, inquiry and trial.

Investigation is the primary stage, which is conducted by the police in which the first information report (FIR) is filed. This stage basically deals with ascertaining facts, establishing the circumstances of the case and collecting evidence. It ends when the charge sheet is made and the police report is sent to the magistrate. Inquiry is the second stage, where the magistrate, on receiving the police sheet, is satisfied with the facts of the case. Trial is the stage where the person is heard in a court of law and is either found guilty or innocent. If any party is aggrieved by the judgment of the trial court, they can approach the High Court and then the Supreme Court. In case a death sentence is confirmed by the Supreme Court, the convict can approach the President of India with a clemency or a mercy petition.

THE ROLE OF THIS BOOK

Media reports often stretch the truth and cloud the facts surrounding a case being decided or already decided by a court of law. On the other hand, reading legal documents to understand how the events really occurred may not be possible for the common man. This book is an attempt to bring to the layperson, one without any specialized knowledge of the law, the true accounts behind several high-profile cases that have

---

[3]A doctrine recognized in *Bachhan Singh vs. State of Punjab*, AIR 1980 SC 898, and subsequently followed by the courts in numerous other cases.

grabbed headlines in the past few years.

Each of these cases has been carefully selected and we have looked into all the available material and facts to arrive at a fairly balanced insight. Special emphasis has been laid on the evidence presented and judgments pronounced in the courts to distinguish between mere allegations and those substantiated by evidence. While selecting the cases for this book, special importance was given to cases which have aroused public interest and have had a substantial effect on the judiciary or the criminal justice system in India. The selected cases showcase all kinds of criminal activity—from terrorism to crimes against women, and white-collar crimes to political murders.

This book, though written by two advocates, is meant for the lay reader and not for those educated in legalese. Efforts have been made to make the references and descriptions of legal procedures as simple and lucid as possible. It must also be stated here that while all reasonable care has been taken to portray the facts as accurately as possible from the materials available, some unforeseen error might have crept in. If any such omission is found, we kindly request the reader to bring it to our attention so that it may be corrected.

DHANANJOY CHATTERJEE:
THE HETAL PAREKH MURDER

*'But secondly you say, "society must exact vengeance, and
society must punish." Wrong on both counts. Vengeance comes
from the individual and punishment from God.'*

—Victor Hugo, *The Last Day of a Condemned Man*

DHANANJOY HAD *'MISTI doi'*[4] and sweets for dinner on 13
August 2004. After dinner, he rested for some time and listened
to some songs by Tagore.[5] In just a few hours, Dhananjoy
Chatterjee would take his last breath. His body remained
hanging for half an hour before the authorized doctors formally
declared him dead. His execution, and the events that preceded
it, created quite a stir in the media and in the minds of the
citizens of India.

The jail officials who were present when Dhananjoy was
serving his prison time stated that Dhananjoy strongly believed
that he would leave the four walls of prison, alive. Pointing to

---

[4]Malabika Bhattacharya, 'Nata Mullick convicted after doing his duty',
The Hindu (Kolkata, 14 August 2004).
[5]Prasanta Paul, 'When the bell tolled for Dhananjoy...was it the end?'
Deccan Herald (Kolkata, 14 August 2004).

his palm, he had once said to a jail official, 'Look, my palm has no line of death, just a line of punishment.'[6] Dhananjoy's family also believed that he would never be executed; they hoped for divine intervention and their belief continued till the very end.[7]

Dhananjoy's confidence in escaping death, however, began to fade when August 2004 arrived, and the date set for his execution crept closer. Jail officials confirmed that he was visibly upset during the last few weeks he spent in prison before he was executed. He had started to believe that he was being executed because he was poor, that he was paying the price of being born into a low income family.

Dhananjoy's family still continued to believe that he would not be executed.[8] His mother regularly performed pujas and prayed to the Almighty to save her beloved son. His wife, whom he had married a month before committing the crime, did everything possible to ensure that her husband was not hanged, despite the fact that he had convinced her to marry him by pretending to work for the border security forces (BSF). She tirelessly spoke to key personnel in the government as well as non-governmental organizations in an attempt to get her husband freed from the shackles of death right until his last moments.[9]

---

[6]Suhrid Sankar Chattopadyay, 'The case of death sentence', *Frontline* (Kolkata, 14-27 August 2004).

[7]Prasanta Paul, 'When the bell tolled for Dhananjoy...was it the end?' *Deccan Herald* (Kolkata, 14 August 2004).

[8]Amit Ukil, 'Hopes pinned on miracle,' *The Telegraph* (Kuludih, 14 August 2004).

[9]Prasanta Paul 'When the bell tolled for Dhananjoy...was it the end?' *Deccan Herald* (Kolkata, 14 August 2004).

When Dhananjoy's family finally came to know that the state had executed him on 14 August 2004 at dawn, they were devastated.[10, 11] Dhananjoy's father said, 'I have been a faithful devotee of Goddess Kali for several years. I hoped there would be a divine intervention at the last moment and my son's life would be saved. Why did the Goddess let me down?'[12] A crowd of people surrounded Dhananjoy's wife and mother, who were inconsolable on hearing the news of his death. On the night following the hanging, there was a deathly silence in Kuludihi, the village in Bankura district of West Bengal, to which Dhananjoy belonged.

THE BEGINNING

Dhananjoy was born into an impoverished family. His father was the village priest. To supplement the family's income, Dhananjoy started working as the security guard of Anand Apartments at Padmapukur in south Kolkata in the beginning of 1990. Nagardas Parekh was a resident in the apartment complex and had a shop on Canning Street in the city. The Parekhs were a happy family. Nagardas' wife was a homemaker and his son, Bhavesh, was a college student and also helped him in business. His daughter, Hetal, was a young fourteen-year-old schoolgirl,[13]

---

[10]'Dhananjoy Chatterjee Hanged in Kolkata Jail', *Indolink* (Kolkata, 14 August 2004).

[11]Kalpana Pradhan, 'Villagers mourn hanged Indian convict', BBC News (Bankura, 14 August 2004).

[12]Malabika Bhattacharya, 'Nata Mullick convicted after doing his duty', *The Hindu* (Kolkata, 14 August 2004).

[13]Hetal Parekh was reported to be fourteen years old at the time of her

bright and fun-loving.

Dhananjoy had been teasing Hetal and harassing her for a while. Distressed, Hetal complained to her mother on 2 March 1990. She said that Dhananjoy regularly teased her when she returned from school. Hetal also told her mother that he had asked her to accompany him to a movie. On hearing this, Hetal's mother immediately informed her husband, who requested the management of the housing society to change the security guard for their complex. Following the orders of the management, on 5 March 1990, Dhananjoy was transferred to the neighbouring Paras Apartments. Bijoy Thapa, another security guard, was deputed in his place.

On 5 March 1990, despite being transferred, Dhananjoy still reported to Anand Apartments. On the same day, at around 1.00 p.m., Hetal returned home after an exam. Dhananjoy, on the pretext of making a telephone call to his supervisor, went into Hetal's apartment between 5.00 and 5.30 p.m. while Hetal was alone at home.

Hetal's mother returned to the apartment after her routine visit to the temple at around 6.00 p.m. She rang the doorbell several times but there was no answer. Sensing that something was wrong, she called the neighbours and begged them for help. Finally, the door was broken open. On entering her apartment, Mrs Parekh's face turned white as she saw her daughter's semi-nude body lying in a pool of blood. Hetal's clothes had been torn, exposing her private parts, and lay scattered all over the

---

death in most news reports. However, the Supreme Court has stated that she was eighteen years old while delivering its final judgment. Hence, extracts from the judgment (given later in the chapter) state that she was eighteen years old.

room. There were dark-red bloodstains on Hetal's hands, head and the clothes she still had on. There was blood on the floor and on the jhoola hanging in the room. With tears rolling down her cheeks, Hetal's mother tenderly picked up her young daughter in her hands as the neighbours formed a shocked circle around them. A doctor was immediately summoned and Hetal was declared dead.

Hetal's father and brother rushed back home on hearing the news. The Parekhs were shattered. Hetal's mother was inconsolable. She could not believe that her darling daughter, whom she had seen smiling a few hours ago, was no longer alive.

INVESTIGATION AND THE LEGAL CASE

Hetal's family informed the police that night about the brutal murder of their daughter. The next morning, the citizens of Kolkata were shocked to hear that such a barbaric incident had taken place in their city. The police began their investigation under intense public scrutiny. On the basis of the circumstantial evidence that the police had unearthed, a case was filed in the trial court against Dhananjoy for the rape and murder of Hetal Parekh.

The additional sessions judge found Dhananjoy guilty of the rape and murder of Hetal after perusing the evidence in great detail and listening to the arguments of the advocates of both the sides. Dhananjoy was sentenced to death by hanging. On appeal, the death sentence passed by the additional sessions judge was confirmed by the Calcutta High Court.

Dhananjoy then filed a special leave petition before the Supreme Court. Dr A.S. Anand and N.P. Singh were the judges who delivered the verdict that Dhananjoy Chatterjee was indeed guilty of the rape and murder of Hetal Parekh. The Supreme Court held that the case was a 'rarest-of-rare' case and sentenced him to capital punishment. It reasoned that the sacred duty of a security guard is to ensure the protection and welfare of the inhabitants of the place where he worked. Dhananjoy had violated this very sacred duty. While delivering the judgment, the Supreme Court observed: 'If the security guards behave in this manner, who will guard the guards?'[14]

It is interesting to note that, in a major move away from tradition, the Supreme Court sentenced Dhananjoy to capital punishment only on the basis of circumstantial evidence. There was no direct evidence to prove that Dhananjoy had actually committed the rape and murder of Hetal Parekh. Also, there were no eyewitnesses who had seen him commit the crime.

Circumstantial evidence refers to the indirect establishment of the existence or non-existence of facts in a criminal or civil litigation. Direct evidence is not easy to present in court, and when it does exist, it is often tampered with by interested parties. Therefore, circumstantial evidence is of great importance in litigation and should not be overlooked.

Circumstantial evidence may be explained with the help of the following example:

If a witness testifies that he saw Ram shooting Hari, this testimony serves as direct evidence and proves that Ram is guilty of murder. However, if the witness says that he saw Hari injured and Ram with a smoking gun at the crime scene, then that becomes circumstantial evidence.

In the landmark case, *Bodh Raj vs. State of Jammu &*

---

[14]Para 16, *Dhananjoy Chatterjee alias Dhana vs. State Of W.B.*, 1994 (1) ALT Cri 388.

Kashmir,[15] the apex court held that circumstantial evidence can be the sole basis for conviction, provided that some conditions such as chain of evidence is complete and the conclusive nature of evidence are fully satisfied.

The Supreme Court held Dhananjoy guilty of the rape and murder of Hetal Parekh on the following grounds: The Supreme Court held that in a case based on circumstantial evidence, the existence of motive plays a significant role. The court held that in the Dhananjoy case, there was ample evidence to show that he had motive to commit the crime. Hetal had been teased by Dhananjoy a number of times on her way to school. Hetal had brought these incidents to the notice of her mother. Hetal had complained to her mother about these incidents just three days before she was raped and killed. Hetal's parents had also acted on her complaints and had requested the housing society to remove Dhananjoy from his post as security guard of the building. The Supreme Court held that there was enough evidence on record to prove that Dhananjoy had had an 'improper attitude' towards Hetal. The Supreme Court also held that Dhananjoy had sufficient motive; the crime could have been committed not only to satisfy his lust and to teach Hetal a lesson for spurning his offer, but also as retaliation for being reported to his employer.

The Supreme Court held that Dhananjoy, being the security guard of Anand Apartments, was aware of the daily routine of the Parekhs. Dhananjoy was aware that Hetal's father and brother had left the apartment early in the morning. Dhananjoy was also aware that Mrs Parekh as a ritual left for the temple every day between 5.00 p.m. and 5.30 p.m. Dhananjoy, being aware of the

---

[15]AIR 2002 SC 3164.

Parekhs' routine, took advantage of the situation and went to the apartment when Hetal was alone. The other security guards at Anand Apartments also testified that they saw Dhananjoy go into the flat. Additionally, on the day of the unfortunate incident, Dhananjoy was seen on the balcony of the Parekhs' apartment.

A cream-coloured button and a chain were recovered from the crime scene. The Supreme Court surmised that there was enough evidence on record to prove that the articles found in the apartment belonged to Dhananjoy.

Immediately after the crime was committed, Dhananjoy went missing. He was finally found on 12 May 1990. The first information report had been recorded by Hetal's family only later that night. Dhananjoy, on the other hand, went missing immediately after the commission of the crime. Dhananjoy's alibi for being missing immediately after Hetal's death was that he had gone to see a movie and had thereafter gone to his native place to participate in his brother's thread ceremony. The Supreme Court held that the alibi advanced by Dhananjoy was not only belated but also vague.

Hetal's mother had informed the police on 6 March 1990, a day after her daughter's death, that a wristwatch had been stolen from their house. The Court held that there was enough evidence to prove that Dhananjoy had sold the same watch that had been stolen from the Parekhs' house.

THE DECISION OF THE SUPREME COURT

The Supreme Court held that Dhananjoy was guilty of the murder and rape of Hetal Parekh, on the basis of circumstantial evidence. It observed that, 'They [the evidence] are specific and of a clinching nature and all of them irresistibly lead to the conclusion that the appellant Dhananjoy was alone guilty of committing rape of Hetal and subsequently murdering her.' The Supreme Court further observed that, 'All the circumstances which have been conclusively established are consistent only with the hypothesis of the guilt of the appellant and are totally inconsistent with his innocence.'[16]

The advocate representing Dhananjoy argued that since Dhananjoy was only twenty-seven years old and had recently got married, he should not be awarded the death penalty. He also argued against the death penalty by claiming that Dhananjoy should be given a chance to become a reformed member of society who learns to respect the dignity of human life.

The Supreme Court stressed the importance of security of women in the country and held that, 'In recent years, the rising crime rate-particularly violent crime against women has made the criminal sentencing by the courts a subject of concern. Today there are admitted disparities. Some criminals get very harsh sentences while many receive grossly different sentence for an essentially equivalent crime and a shockingly large number even go unpunished, thereby encouraging the criminal and in the ultimate making justice suffer by weakening the system's credibility. Of course, it is not possible to lay down any cut and dry formula relating to imposition of sentence but the object of sentencing should be to see that the crime does not go unpunished and the victim of crime as also the society has the satisfaction that justice has been done to it.'[17]

---

[16]Para 7, *Dhananjoy Chatterjee Alias Dhana vs. State Of W.B*, 1994 (1) ALT Cri 388.

[17]Para 14, *Dhananjoy Chatterjee Alias Dhana vs. State Of W.B*, 1994 (1) ALT Cri 388.

It held that the death penalty was justified in the case as the victim was a helpless fourteen-year-old girl and Dhananjoy's acts were motivated by lust and revenge. The Supreme Court observed, '[...] should have subjected the deceased, a resident of one of the flats, to gratify his lust and murder her in retaliation for his transfer on her complaint, makes the crime even more heinous. Keeping in view the medical evidence and the state in which the body of the deceased was found, it is obvious that a most heinous type of barbaric rape and murder was committed on a helpless and defenceless school-going girl of eighteen years.'

The Supreme Court ended the judgment with these last few lines, 'The offence was not only inhuman and barbaric, but it was a totally ruthless crime of rape followed by cold-blooded murder and an affront to the human dignity of the society [...] We agree that a real and abiding concern for the dignity of human life is required to be kept in mind by the courts while considering the confirmation of the sentence of death but a cold-blooded pre-planned brutal murder, without any provocation, after committing rape on an innocent and defenceless young girl of eighteen years by the security guard certainly makes this case a "rare of the rarest" case which calls for no punishment other than the capital punishment and we accordingly confirm the sentence of death imposed upon the appellant for the offence [...]'

Dhananjoy was finally awarded the death sentence by the Supreme Court, which also found support in the media. Dhananjoy's family had petitioned many times for presidential pardon between the years 1994 and 2004. On 25 June 2004, the then president, A.P.J. Abdul Kalam, reviewed Dhananjoy's mercy petition and sought the state government's view on the matter. The ruling Left Front government made it very clear that it supported the death penalty in the case. Chief Minister Buddhadeb Bhattacharjee said, 'The government and I are in favour of the death sentence in this particular case. The Centre should be informed of this. The message should go loud and clear to the perpetrators of such crime.' Dhananjoy's mercy petition was rejected by president Kalam.

Dhananjoy was hanged to death on 14 August 2004. Nata Mallick, the executioner who was present during the last few minutes before Dhananjoy's life came to an end, said that he had been a part of many executions but the most painful among them had been the execution of Dhananjoy Chatterjee. When Nata Mallik put the black hood over Dhananjoy's head and tightened the noose around his neck, he said, 'Dhananjoy, please forgive me for what I am going to do. I am just carrying out what the sarkar (government) and the court ordered me to do. Hume maaf kar do.'[18] Dhananjoy maintained that he was innocent and had not committed the crime of rape or murder of Hetal Parekh, till the very last moment. He muttered these words when the black cloth was put on him, 'I would like all of you to know I am innocent and I am going without justice. I have no malice, no ill feelings towards any one of you.'[19]

Dhananjoy Chatterjee was the fifty-fifth person to be executed in Indian since independence. The execution was one of the most publicized cases in the history of the criminal justice system of India. It took place nine years after the execution of Auto Shankar in 1995 and evoked mixed reactions from the

---

[18]'Dhananjoy pleaded innocence till last: Hangman', Rediff News (Kolkata, 14 August 2004).

[19]Ibid and 'Dhananjoy's last words: I am innocent', *Times of India* (Kolkata, 15 August 2004).

people of India, especially the people of Kolkata. While most people agreed that Dhananjoy's act of rape and murder of an innocent young girl deserved the death sentence, many others did not think that he deserved to die such a miserable death after having served fourteen years behind bars.

AUTHORS' NOTE

The criminal justice system in our country has evolved out of observing the law systems in other countries. The test for conviction for even the most heinous offences has been that the guilt of the accused must be established 'beyond reasonable doubt'. Parallel trials by the media, like it happened in the present case, pose a real threat to the objectivity of the trial judge. Judges cannot be isolated from society. As the saying goes, no man is an island. Therefore, in spite of their objective training and thinking, it is conceivable that even trial judges can be subconsciously influenced by societal pressures. On the other hand, we must also acknowledge the very real contribution of the media in a country like India where there is a great need for awareness among all sections of society regarding crimes against women.

However, the Dhananjoy case was an extreme occurrence where the media became frenzied and convicted the man with the zeal of a lynch mob, at times ignoring the fact that the entire case was solely based on circumstantial evidence. There was no way of saying with any certainty that Dhananjoy was definitely guilty of raping and murdering the victim. This criticism does mean that convictions cannot or should not happen solely on the basis of circumstantial evidence. A case such as this one has a high degree of legal complexity and the Indian media could have exhibited greater sensitivity, especially since unfavourable coverage risks prejudicing society against the defendant and can affect the lives of those who were close to the accused.

In the course of this book, we will see how the Indian media has become increasingly active in the arena of crime reporting and has shaped the views of society regarding various cases. There is no denying that this role falls within the core objectives of the media. However, this book will trace the evolution of this kind of crime coverage in India and will show that the increase in this kind of activism is influenced by many factors and is not just driven by a sense of duty or journalistic freedom, as it is often believed.

SANTOSH KUMAR SINGH: THE PRIYADARSHINI MATTOO MURDER

'Beauty provokes harassment, the law says, but it looks through men's eyes when deciding what provokes it.'

—Naomi Wolf, *The Beauty Myth: How Images of Beauty Are Used Against Women*

CHAMAN MATTOO RETURNED to his house at Vasant Kunj, Delhi, at about 7.30 p.m. on 23 January 1996, to find that a large crowd had gathered there. When he walked into the house, he found his daughter lying in the bedroom with blood oozing from her mouth; she had been raped and murdered. The Mattoo family were devastated to find their bright, beautiful daughter brutally murdered in their own home. It would take fourteen long years for the murderer of Priyadarshini Mattoo to be brought to justice.

When Rajeshwari Mattoo came home later that evening and saw her daughter's lifeless body, she went into shock. She immediately knew who had done it—the man who had harassed and molested her daughter for almost two years; against whom several police complaints had been filed to no avail; a stalker who escaped every time with useless vows of good behaviour; the man whose conduct had cornered her daughter into getting a Personal Security Officer (PSO)—the accused, Santosh Kumar Singh.

Priyadarshini had completed her bachelor's degree in commerce in Jammu before moving to Delhi with her family. They were one of the thousands of Kashmiri Pandit families forced to flee the Valley due to an increase in terrorist activity. She was one of three children, but the only one living with her parents in 1996—her brother and sister were in Canada. Priyadarshini enrolled at Delhi University to study law in 1992. She was determined to become an IAS officer.

Priyadarshini had only just started college when she met Santosh Kumar, her senior, who was the son of a police inspector. Right from the beginning, things didn't go well. He developed an obsessive attraction for her, while she had only disdain for him. Even after he graduated, he was often seen on his motorbike, stalking her in college and outside, stopping her car and tormenting her. He gave her flowers, grabbed her by the hand and followed her around. Santosh Kumar went so far as to propose to Priyadarshini. He even tried to break into her home on one occasion.

However, Priyadarshini was a strong, independent and confident young woman, and she acted with great resolve and determination. She did everything in her power to dissuade Santosh Kumar. She filed five separate complaints against him at various police stations in Delhi. When this didn't work, as a last resort, she went with her father to speak to the superintendent of police. For her security, she was given a PSO, Rajinder Singh. Her PSO was expected to be by her side at all times. This was the most that could be done in the situation—but it was not enough. Unable to stand the rejection, Santosh Kumar hunted her down in her own house and killed her. Dubbed a 'crime of passion', the brutal rape and murder of Priyadarshini Mattoo shocked the entire nation.

Continuous complaints, since the beginning of 1995, were not acted upon by the State. When it did react, the State with all its power was unable to stop Santosh Kumar Singh. On 23 January 1996, Priyadarshini was found in her house with severe damage to her face. She had suffered nineteen injuries and three broken ribs. Blood pooled around her. There was a cord of a heat convector wrapped around her neck, which Santosh Kumar had used to strangle her. It was clear that she had been raped. An instant of inhumane brutality had abruptly ended the life and journey of Priyadarshini.

When the news of her murder broke the next day, the nation went into a state of shock. This to-be lawyer was known to be friendly and confident. She could play the guitar and was a good singer. She could have been anybody's daughter or anybody's friend. The discovery of this ruthless crime sent tremors of fear all over India, especially in the north. Delhi had a reputation for crimes against women, and the crime rate in the city was only mounting. Vasant Kunj was an upper-middle-class residential area, whose great walls and posse of guards had once been a guarantee of safety in the 1980s. All those safety measures had proved futile against a student of law. Priyadarshini had taken every precaution possible—including having a personal security officer guard her. So, why had it not been enough to ensure her safety, and why had the police been so helpless?

The most disturbing fact about this crime is not that the precautionary measures had failed—but that Santosh had not been stopped earlier only because he was the son of highly valued police officer, J.P. Singh. The laxity and weak will of the Delhi police had enabled him to commit this crime. Santosh Kumar was a man who should have been put in jail, on the basis of any one of the five complaints that had been made, in spite of which he received chance after a chance, and unfortunately, one chance too many. This case is enough to make one believe that holding an important position in India guarantees one and one's relatives immunity against anything they may do, even murder.

THE DAY OF THE CRIME

Before

Priyadarshini left for college with her parents on the morning of 23 January 1996 at around 9.15 a.m., as her PSO was late and could not accompany her. Santosh Kumar was noticed by the PSO that morning at the Delhi University campus law centre, with his bike and helmet both in good condition. Later that day, Priyadarshini returned home with Rajinder Singh, and told him to come back at around 5.30 p.m. At around 4.50 p.m., Kuppuswamy (a neighbour) noticed Santosh Kumar standing outside her house. In the evening, Priyadarshini purchased some plastic goods from a street vendor, establishing the fact that she was at home. A little while later, her servant, Virender Prasad, left to visit his friend. At 4.55 p.m., he returned only to take the dog out and to go buy some medication. It was then that Priyadarshini was completely alone at home.

During

Reports state that Santosh Kumar had gone to her house to apologize, to ask for forgiveness for the way he had behaved in the past and to tell her that it was over. He pleaded with her to let him inside. Believing the note of sincerity in his voice, Priyadarshini let him enter. However, like every other vow he had made in the past, this just turned out to be another false promise. One minute he was begging her for forgiveness, and the next he was proposing yet again. Priyadarshini was scared since there was no one else in the house. In the face of his repeated and aggressive attempts to persuade her, Priyadarshini asked him to leave, telling him that there never had been, nor was, nor would there ever be, any reciprocation from her. Unable to take rejection once more, he seized the opportunity, threw her down and forced himself upon her. He raped her and to stifle the sound of her crying, began battering her face with his helmet. He hit her repeatedly until her face became unrecognizable after nineteen injuries. There was blood everywhere and broken bits of glass from his helmet visor were strewn around the room. He then grabbed the closest thing he could find—the heat convector cord—and strangled her.

After

The PSO, along with Constable Dev Kumar, reached Priyadarshini's residence at 5.30 p.m. There was no answer when they rang the doorbell. They then decided to check the door that gave access to the house from the side of the courtyard. They knocked and realized that it was open. Inside, they found Priyadarshini lying under the bed. They immediately made a call to the Vasant Kunj police station and informed them of the incident. The following is a part of the report translated into English:

'On arrival at the house, Priyadarshini Mattoo was lying under the double bed placed in the bedroom of the house and her body showed no movement. It appears that some incident has occurred [...][20]

At about 5.30 p.m., after the crime had been committed, Santosh Kumar was seen near the residence by Jaideep Singh Ahluwalia, the area security supervisor (Prosecution Witness 3). Santosh had a class soon after, for which he arrived a few minutes late.

THE JUDGMENT

Santosh Kumar was booked under sections 376 and 302 of the Indian Penal Code, for rape and murder. The additional sessions judge, S.C. Mittal, framed charges on 17 July 1997. Santosh Kumar was acquitted by the sessions court on 3 December 1999, due to insufficient evidence. An appeal to the Delhi High Court was admitted on 29 February 2000, and after six years, the court ruled that Santosh Kumar was guilty and awarded him the death penalty on 17 October 2006. The High Court held that its sentence was based on the sufficient evidence produced by India's premier investigative agency, the Central Bureau of Investigation (CBI) and that the lower court's judgment had been perverse. The accused appealed to the Supreme Court, the highest judicial power in the country, on 19 February 2007. The Supreme Court, while pronouncing him guilty on both counts, reduced his sentence to life imprisonment, on 6 October 2012.[21] The Supreme Court's decision to mitigate the sentence was largely based on Santosh's position as a parent and husband, in addition to the fact that his father had passed away in the intervening years after the High Court's verdict. The

---

[20]*State (Through CBI) vs. Santosh Kumar Singh*, 2007 CriLJ 964.

[21]*Santosh Kumar Singh vs. State through CBI*, [2010] 9 SCC 747.

death penalty may only be given in the 'rarest of rare' cases in India and the Supreme Court did not consider this case as such.

This became a landmark case because on the same facts, circumstances, and most importantly, the same evidence, the sessions court acquitted the accused, the High Court sentenced him to death, and the Supreme Court commuted his sentence to life imprisonment.

Before examining the judgment of each court, it would be useful to take a look at the evidence presented before the court.

THE CIRCUMSTANTIAL EVIDENCE OF THE CASE

The incidents that took between 4.55 p.m.-5.30 p.m. on 23 January 1996 had no eyewitnesses since the crime took place in Priyadarshini's bedroom, where no one but her and the accused were present. Only circumstantial evidence was available. Therefore, through indirect facts, the prosecution had to establish the sequence of events to convince the courts.

In criminal justice it is essential that all the evidence available forms a chain of events that will unambiguously lead to one definite conclusion. Successful prosecution is possible only if such a definite conclusion can be reached beyond reasonable doubt.

The circumstantial evidence available in this case pointed towards one possibility—that of Santosh Kumar Singh's guilt. The evidence available stacked up as follows:

The neighbour, Kuppuswamy, noticed Santosh Kumar Singh standing outside Priyadarshini's residence, near the door towards the staircase, immediately prior to the commission of the crime at approximately 4.50 p.m. with the visor of his helmet still intact. Jaideep Singh Ahluwalia, the security supervisor, also saw the accused at about 5.30 p.m. near the victim's residence. Santosh

Kumar was noticed leaving the B-10 Vasant Kunj area around 5.30 p.m. by O.P. Singh, an advocate.

- Singh arrived late for his class on 23 January 1996, which might prove that he had been at Priyadarshini's house.
- The state in which Priyadarshini's body had been left in, including the condition of her clothes, the cord around her neck, bloodstains, scratches, etc., showed that there had been a struggle and force had been used to overpower her. Additionally, blood samples further tied Santosh Kumar Singh to the crime scene.
- The medical check-up of Santosh Kumar Singh evinced damage to his hand and eyes.
- Kuppuswamy guaranteed that the helmet visor was intact just prior to the commission of the crime, but it was seen broken afterwards.
- The accused had stalked and threatened Priyadarshini for a year-and-a-half before the commission of the crime.

It is on the interpretation of the above evidence that the courts decided on the innocence or guilt of the accused.

SESSIONS COURT

The sessions court judge acquitted the accused of rape under Section 376 of the Indian Penal Code, and extended the benefit of doubt for murder under Section 302.

The additional sessions judge, Justice Thareja, declared in open court that the court knew that the accused was responsible for the rape and murder of Priyadarshini, but was forced to set him free on reasonable doubt. He said that it had no option as insufficient evidence had been presented to convict the accused.

This sensational acquittal sparked nationwide protests. Women's organizations, parliamentarians and students' groups spearheaded the campaign against the verdict. It was impossible to digest that so clear a case had been dismissed with such totality. There was outrage that Santosh Kumar Singh had been released as a free man. There were several rallies and marches. Pamphlets were distributed and the parliament discussed the mishandling of the case by the CBI and the Delhi police in one of its debates.

The CBI's report indicated lapses in the investigation conducted by the Delhi police. News reports about the CBI's confidential internal report indicated that the Delhi police had attempted to shield the accused[22]. It is important to note that Santosh Kumar Singh's father had been the joint commissioner of the Delhi police at the time of the investigation. However, no role in the alleged shielding of the accused has been attributed to him.

The crime had exposed how vulnerable civil society is, and how difficult it is to ensure justice in the aftermath of such a ghastly offence. Citizens began rallying to the cause, believing that if they didn't act and raise their voices, such criminals would continue on their rampage unstopped.

The sessions court rejected key pieces of evidence that were presented by the CBI and held that the proposed chain of events was not fully established leaving room for the possibility of the innocence of the accused. The CBI brought to the notice of the court that the defendant's hand was injured. Through the testimonies of the personal security officer and Kuppuswamy, it

---

[22]Siddhartha Sarma, 'Mattoo story revisited', *The Indian Express* (21 July 2006).

attempted to establish that Santosh's helmet had been intact just prior to the incident at 5.00 p.m., but was broken afterwards. The accused stated that the injury as well as the damage to the helmet was the result of an accident which had occurred on 14 January 1996 and not on 23 January. Although the court had admitted these testimonies, it allowed that the accident on the 14 January 1996 might have been a possibility.

Further, the DNA tests, which had proved conclusively that Priyadarshini had been raped, were declared inadmissible by the trial court. It believed that there was a possibility that the material sent for the DNA tests had been tampered with. It went on to state that the test procedure was not fair and proper and was carried out by experts who were incompetent.

Even though the court admitted a part of the evidence, including the motive of the accused, the complaints filed by Priyadarshini at various police stations, the presence of the accused around Priyadarshini's house immediately prior to and post the commission of the crime, it was not enough to prove the case beyond 'reasonable doubt' as required for a conviction.

Finally, the sessions court gave the benefit of doubt to the accused on the grounds that:

- There was a lack of fair play on the part of CBI.
- The CBI was blamed for the absence of the key witness, Virender Singh, the domestic help of the deceased. Even though there were several attempts by the CBI to bring forth the said witness, he could not be traced.
- The sessions court, in favour of prosecution, has itself recorded that no adverse inference can be drawn against the prosecution for not examining Virender Singh.

Chaman Lal Mattoo, who had been awaiting the judgment on

his daughter's case, attended court religiously, adjournment after adjournment, date after date. His attendance was so regular that the trial court judge was prompted to tell him that there was no real need for him to come to court for every session; he would hear of the judgment in due time.

Chaman Lal Mattoo on 3 December 1999 received a call that shattered him. His four-year-long wait for justice for his daughter had been in vain. His daughter's rapist and murderer was set free. His wife was abroad at the time; he called her and wept. There was a great sense of defeat and overbearing grief. He cried to his relatives, 'My faith in the Almighty has been shaken. How will I be able to face Priyadarshini in heaven?'[23] They had waited and waited for some relief from the ordeal that had begun on the 23 January 1996, but the system had failed. He resolved to fight the case till the bitter end and decided to file an appeal.

It is a well-known fact that people with power and influence are treated better than the common man in our country. This is so common that it has become part of our everyday reality and no longer carries the label of 'corruption'. However, this time an invisible line had been crossed; immunity for murder and rape was unacceptable. This was not a single occurrence; it threatened to repeat itself—Jessica Lal was murdered as brutally on 30 April 1999. The son of a politician, for no fault of hers, shot her, in the middle of a party. These two cases are startlingly similar—girls who came from middle-class families were killed brutally by men in power and the perpetrators were obvious to everyone, including the courts. The first courts to hear both cases acquitted the accused.

---

[23]'Chaman Lal Mattoo up close', *The Indian Express* (19 October 2006).

The CBI was squarely blamed for the unfavourable judgment by the public, especially since the trial court had pointed out several flaws in their investigation. The trial court had gained much public sympathy by stating that although they knew that Santosh Kumar Singh was guilty, the lack of evidence forced them to acquit him. 'The judiciary is shocked by what the trial court judge in the Priyadarshini case said, so this is a historical judgment[24],' said an activist Aditya Raj Kaul.

It was only later that the Delhi High Court provided the view that the trial court was wrong in delivering a perverse judgment.

HIGH COURT

The CBI filed an appeal before the Delhi High Court on 29 February 2000, but there was no action taken until 2006. In March 2006, the Jessica Lal case was reopened, which breathed new life into the Priyadarshini Mattoo case as well. On Priyadarshini's birth anniversary, on 24 July 2006, a candlelight march was organized—civil rights activists, members of various social organizations, former union minister Maneka Gandhi, actor Anupam Kher, and United Students, a Delhi University students' group, got involved. Text messages, pamphlets, posters and emails were circulated to raise awareness. The protesters were united by a common case—they believed that 'The State must fulfil its obligations, and if it can't, then we have no right to pretend that we have a justice system at all.'[25]

---

[24]'Matto case: Media take a bow?', *IBN Live* (New Delhi, 18 October 2006).

[25]'Re-trial demanded in Priyadarshini case', *The Hindu* (New Delhi, 24 July 2006).

The CBI faced criticism for letting the case slide for seven years from the date of the acquittal in the trial court, and they in turn filed an application in the Delhi High Court to fast track the proceedings. The court, making a rare exception, declared day-to-day hearings. The trial went on for forty-two days and the court delivered its verdict on 17 October 2006, finding Santosh Kumar guilty of the crimes he had committed.

The High Court held Santosh Kumar Singh guilty on both counts of rape and murder and sentenced him to death on 30 October 2006. Justice Sodhi and Justice Bhasin, the judges who heard this case, patted the CBI on the back for proving Santosh's guilt 'beyond any doubt by unimpeachable evidence'.

The High Court accepted the DNA tests presented by the CBI, which proved the rape of Priyadarshini. The court noted that it would be dangerous for the judiciary to fall into the convention of discarding the evidence of an expert witness by referring to certain texts and books without putting those texts to the expert and taking his opinion thereon.

With respect to Santosh Kumar's alleged accident on 14 January 1996—which was presented by him as the cause of the fifth metacarpal hand injury and the damage to the visor of the helmet—the High Court held that this accident was not plausible and that the helmet did not show any visible signs of the accident. More importantly, the accused was required to prove this accident. He was required to produce hospital records proving the date and nature of the injury, but these records were never submitted. Also, none of the doctors who had diagnosed him were examined. The High Court greatly criticized the decision of the sessions court to reject the evidence of the hand injury and the broken helmet on flimsy grounds.

Both the courts, however, agreed that the Delhi police had exhibited lax behaviour in dealing with Priyadarshini's complaints prior to 23 January 1996. On 28 September 2006, the court is noted to have said to the police, 'the girl has died because of you not the boy,' and that, 'the girl has gone on and on bearing this onslaught,' and, 'what kind of police do we have in this town where no one is safe?'[26]

This verdict seemed like a victory for the whole nation, which had been brought together for this cause by the media, which had played a very active role in getting the case re-opened and bringing attention to the injustice of the acquittal. Since the case was covered across television, print and online media, escalating pressure from the public was instrumental in fast tracking this case. 'Without media, I don't think the so-called conscience of judiciary would have woken up. It took six years for the judiciary, what happened in the intervening years?'[27] asks editor-in-chief of the news weekly *Outlook*, Vinod Mehta.

The death sentence by the High Court proved that the nation had not turned apathetic and slumped completely into complacency after sixty years of corruption and trivialization of the justice system. The verdict was a testimony to the power of the youth as well, who had rallied and played a vital role in pushing the case through court.

---

[26]'HC reserves verdict in Mattoo murder case', *DNA* (New Delhi, 27 September 2006).

[27]'Matto case: Media take a bow?', *IBN Live* (New Delhi, 18 October 2006).

SUPREME COURT

Santosh Kumar Singh appealed against the verdict of the High Court to the Supreme Court, on 19 February 2007. In what many considered to be a grave injustice, the Supreme Court, although it held Santosh Kumar guilty of rape and murder, commuted his sentence from death to life imprisonment on 6 October 2012.

Rajeshwari Mattoo, who had left the country soon after the commission of the crime, was vocal for the first time. According to her, it was incumbent upon her to raise the awareness about the injustice meted out to her daughter and the crimes committed against women. 'I chose to remain silent for the first thirteen years because as a mother I found it unbearable to speak about it in the public,' she said.[28] She said that she felt like she was reliving the rape and murder of her daughter with this sentence. She firmly believed that Santosh could not be reformed. According to her, if he had been capable of reforming, then her daughter would have still been alive.

The Supreme Court believed that this was not a rarest of rare case. Santosh's life was spared because his father had died after the judgment of the High Court and he had married in the intermittent four years between the judgment of the High Court and that of the Supreme Court, and had a daughter. Furthermore, the Supreme Court was of the belief that there was a chance that he may reform, and to uphold the death sentence would deal a fatal blow to his young family.

---

[28]'"Disillusioned" with judicial system: Priyadarshini's mother', *The Indian Express* (Srinagar, 9 August 2011).

AUTHORS' NOTE

The Priyadarshini Mattoo and Jessica Lal cases were, in many ways, watershed moments in the history and evolution of the Indian media. Electronic media, in particular, played a pivotal role in establishing a strong emotional connect with its viewers. Outside the purview of the law, the Indian media played a very crucial and impactful role in ensuring that the offenders did not escape by misusing their power and wealth to subvert investigative agencies or the prosecutorial system. In the end, one can safely say that in the Priyadarshini Mattoo case, justice prevailed. While there have been other instances where the media was criticized for either sensationalizing news or keeping selectively silent, in this case, it effectively mobilized civil groups and brought the accused to justice. This case will long be remembered and recognized as a feather in the cap of the Indian media.

AJMAL KASAB: THE 26/11 MUMBAI ATTACK AND AFTER

'This was not an act of terrorism, it was an act of war.'

—George W. Bush

'HIMMAT KARNI HAI mere veer, ghabraana nahin hai, Insha-allah, goli lagey toh kaamyaabi hai Allah intezaar kar raha hai... [29]

These eerie words were uttered by an unknown faceless voice, a collaborator across the western border, to a terrorist in the Oberoi Trident Hotel in Mumbai—telling him not to fear being hit by a bullet because God is waiting to receive him.

Ajmal Kasab and nine of his comrades entered Mumbai on 26 November 2008 with the aim of taking lives. Terrorists, mainly operating from Pakistan, engineered the attack which resulted tragically in the murder of 166 people. The young men had been lured into working for Lashkar-e-Taiba with money and the promise that they were fighting a jihad, a holy war against the enemies of Islam. Thus, by twisting the tenets of Islam, these harbingers of death and destruction raised their army of youth, whose sole motive was to kill and die.

However, for one of the ten terrorists, things did not go

---

[29]Transcripts From Hotel Oberoi Talk No. 4 (Ext. No. 979).

according to plan. Ajmal Kasab was caught alive and was arrested by the Mumbai police on 27 November 2008. Photographs of his youthful face were splashed across news channels and newspapers. The immaturity of his face stood in strong contrast against the automatic rifle he held in his hands—the same rifle that he had used to mow down innumerable innocent people. He was tried and convicted for criminal conspiracy and for waging war on the nation. The sessions court for Greater Mumbai sentenced him to death, which was later upheld by the Bombay High Court and Supreme Court.

FROM PAKISTAN WITH LOVE

Very rarely has a criminal conspiracy shaken the fabric of a nation in recent memory like this massacre did. Like the 9/11 terror attacks in the USA, this was also a meticulously planned conspiracy by terrorists across the border with the aim of causing maximum damage and panic in India. The total number of accused was forty-four.

Kasab was born in the dusty village of Faridkot in a remote and impoverished region of Punjab in Pakistan's farming belt. Home to 10,000 people, most of the inhabitants of Faridkot are farmers and labourers and literacy is low. Kasab's father, Mohammed Amir Iman, ran a food stall in the village.

In 2000, Kasab dropped out of his Urdu-medium school when he was thirteen years old. A year later, he went with his father in search of greener pastures to Lahore. He worked as a labourer for the next five years. His new source of income, and the independence that came with it, caused rifts between him and his father. He moved to a new job at Welcome Tent Services, which introduced him to others like him, without educational qualifications or any direction in life. One Muzaffar Lal Khan became his close friend and confidante. Both Kasab and Muzaffar, being dissatisfied by their current position, moved to Rawalpindi to seek better luck.

It was there that they came in contact with the Lashkar-e-Taiba. The terrorist organization gave their vagabond lives a purpose, and without a job or a home to root them, they soaked it up. The words of firebrand Muslim clerics and leaders brainwashed them into believing that the most noble and patriotic act that they could do was lay down their lives for their religion—jihad. They listened to speeches and stories, and their young minds inflamed with hatred towards their enemies they were taught to despise—like India, USA and Israel. The lure of substantial money for them and their family also helped to make up the minds of these dissatisfied and jobless youth. Without a guardian or a voice of reason to warn them, Kasab and Muzaffar became jihadis in December 2007.

They were not concerned by the fact that jihad would mean the slaughter of hundreds of innocents, people whom they did not know. There was no one to tell them that a path slippery with blood cannot lead to the garden of heaven. They were blind to the fact they were mere pawns meant to be sacrificed in a larger political game of chess.

A series of training sessions—*Daura-e-Duffa, Daura-e-Amma* and *Daura-e-Khassa*—beginning in December 2007, converted these young boys into trained killers. Their mentors or Ameers, as they were called, trained them in the various skills they would need for such missions. They were praised for their abilities to kill and destroy. They were told that everything was fair when it came to jihad, because it was in the name of Allah.

Kasab's friend Muzaffar was saved by his brother who took

him away during the training period. No one came for Kasab. His resolve strengthened and he survived through the toughest training sessions—he hiked steep mountainous terrains and went for long periods of time without food. After the final training sessions, his ameer gave him ₹1,300 to go home for a week. Kasab went back home and sought blessings from his mother. He was going for jihad, he said.

In the meantime, the organization chalked out the plan down to the minutest details. On 13 November 2008, the ones chosen for the mission were told that the time for jihad had arrived. They were to attack Mumbai by sea. They were to weaken Hindustan by causing death and destruction in the financial capital of the country.

The ten selected terrorists were divided into *buddiyas*, or pairs. Each pair was to attack a different location, and each location was picked meticulously. The aim was to kill a large number of people, citizens from around the globe, especially Jews. The locations chosen were the Chhatrapati Shivaji Terminus (CST), Café Leopold, the Oberoi Trident Hotel at Nariman Point, The Taj Mahal Palace at the Gateway of India and Nariman House.

The terrorists set sail on a hijacked boat, wearing yellow threads on their wrists and carrying fake ID cards with Hindu names to blend into the crowd. They killed everyone on the boat except the navigator who, they thought, would prove useful in directing the boat through the sea and into the dock carefully.

Throughout the training, the ameers and the trainees had become like a family where everyone was trusted, and every word was obeyed. However, as the plan unravelled, the relationship between the main organization and the terrorists became clear. The constant voice in their ear told them repeatedly not to fear getting shot and that, under no circumstances, were they to be arrested by the police. During these conversations, the Lashkar-e-Taiba seemed displeased to hear that the terrorists had failed to cover their tracks effectively. They had left the hijacked boat afloat. They had reached late and had forgotten their GPS devices in the boat. The ten terrorists were told to get the attention of the media, but they were not informed till the last minute about what their demands were.

It would have no doubt given the masterminds behind this attack great displeasure to hear that not only was Kasab caught, but he had revealed every detail he knew about the training and the planning of the attack in his voluntary confession.

THE NIGHT MUMBAI BLED

On the night of 26 November 2008 they reached the shores of Mumbai, at Badhwar Park, on the stolen vessel. Once the destination was reached, the navigator became a burden and also a liability who knew too much. Kasab ruthlessly slit the navigator's or nakhava's neck and they abandoned the boat.

Kasab and his partner Ismail were the first to get a taxi. They planted a bomb under the taxi driver's seat, set to go off in one hour and fifteen minutes. Both of them were designated to reach CST at 7.30 p.m. and create 'piles of bodies'.

CST

On reaching the station, Kasab and Ismail realized that they were two hours late and had missed the rush hour. The videos that they had seen during training, of throngs of people rushing into trains, did not materialize. The piles of bodies they had envisioned were not to be. Confused and disappointed, they tried to reach their mentors in Pakistan, but they were unable to get through. Eager to put their training to the test, they decided to kill as many as they could. They launched a grenade into the waiting room and pulled out their guns to start indiscriminate firing. They moved from the long-distance-train platforms to the local-train platforms and killed everyone in sight and everything that moved. Soon the station was empty, but it was not without fight.

The duo met several policemen along their way who laid down their lives as they valiantly attempted to save lives and secure the station premises. Unfortunately, their equipment and training were no match for the terrorists who feared nothing and killed without hesitation. The announcement booth was quick to react in the face of the carnage. The announcers immediately began guiding people away from the havoc. Dodging bullets and hiding below the counter, they informed people of the assault and instructed the passengers descending from trains to use the rear exit. This act of courage standing in the line of fire saved many lives that day.

A surreal atmosphere enveloped the station. The heart of the Mumbai train network, which carries thousands of people every day, from home to school, college, work and back, had never before witnessed such a ghastly scene.

On hearing the shots fired at CST, two journalists from the *Times of India* rushed over with nothing but their cameras in their hands. They managed to capture the entire attack as it unfurled before their eyes. They fearlessly put themselves in harm's way to take photos of the slaughter. Luckily, they lived to tell the tale through their photos. Several images of the terrorists were collected from their two cameras and this evidence played an important role in Kasab's conviction.

Kasab and Ismail managed to exit the station. According to the plan, their next destination was supposed to be Malabar Hill.

Meanwhile, terror was simultaneously unleashed at Café Leopold (11 killed, 28 injured), the Taj Mahal Palace (36 killed, 30 injured), Nariman House (9 killed, 7 injured) and the Oberoi Trident Hotel (35 killed, 24 injured) between 9.15 p.m. and 9.55 p.m. All of these locations were very close to each other, so it was possible for the terrorists to walk over and assist one another.

Café Leopold

Café Leopold is a popular watering hole in south Mumbai. It is always crowded with young people, both Indians and foreigners. The crowd and the presence of a large international clientele made it an ideal location for the attack. Shoaib and Nazir Ahmad, the second '*buddiya*', took a taxi to their point of attack. Since Café Leopold was a small and closed space, it took mere minutes to wreck the restaurant with grenades and AK-47s. The boisterous and jolly place instantaneously turned into a bloody mess. Shoaib and Nazir quickly left, and began walking to The Taj Mahal Palace hotel.

The Taj Mahal Palace Hotel

Abdul Rehman and Javed targetted The Taj Mahal Palace hotel, one of the most luxurious hotels in India and a landmark building in Mumbai. Shoaib and Nazir joined the duo soon after. The Taj was chosen for many reasons. It was one of the most glorious buildings in the city, frequented by the wealthy and influential. Also, it saw a vast number of international guests. To set it aflame would send a clear message. Throughout the horrific episode, the terrorists and their mentors from Pakistan seemed strangely obsessed with setting the place on fire. They were specifically instructed time and again to set the dome of the Taj alight. The photo of the burning Taj, splashed all over the media, became symbolic of the destruction that the terrorists had caused, but at the same time, it strengthened the resolve of the Indians to rise above this horrific carnage.

After showering bullets into the lobby, the terrorists went up the stairs and took hostages. They burnt beds, curtains and whatever else they could find. This proved unsuccessful and the rooms filled up with so much smoke that the terrorists themselves were forced to leave the floor temporarily. Some of the hostages used this opportunity to escape through the windows. After a long and hard gun battle with the police and other security forces, the terrorists at the Taj were the last to be killed, on the morning of 29 November 2008.

Nariman House

Nariman House is a residential-cum-prayer house used by Israelis for temporary accommodation. Imran Babar and Nasir was the pair that attacked it. The place was chosen due to the hatred that the terrorists had towards Israelis. They believed that Israel had unjustly persecuted Muslims for decades and therefore wanted revenge. When the people inside were taken hostage, there was an attempt to negotiate, but eventually they killed most of them.

The Oberoi Trident Hotel

The Oberoi Trident was the last point of attack by Fahadulla and Abdul Rehman a.k.a., Chhota, who arrived there by boat at 9.55 p.m. They entered the hotel and started firing indiscriminately, destroying the lobby and killing diners at Tiffin, the in-house restaurant. The staff of Khamdar, another restaurant on the mezzanine, noticed the firing and quickly bolted their front doors and escorted the guests out of the service exit. When the terrorists reached Khamdar, they were disappointed to find only two staff members. One of the staff members was shot and killed, but the other managed to escape.

The terrorists ensured that they set the building on fire. They moved upwards, through each floor, setting the place on fire. At times, they themselves would have to back out due to the intensity of the fire and smoke. Some guests managed to escape through the windows. However, the terrorists killed others and took several as hostages. The commandoes of the National Security Guard (NSG) killed the terrorists at the Oberoi Trident on the morning of 28 November 2008, at around 7 a.m.

Even as chaos erupted in south Mumbai across these locations, Kasab and Ismail came under heavy gunfire outside CST. While trying to find a car or any means of transport to get to the next destination, they were fired at heavily by the police. They returned fire and hid in the next building—Cama Hospital. The gun battle continued between the police and the terrorists for some time, and several policemen were killed. The terrorists would not have hesitated to kill as many people as possible in the hospital as well, but the quick thinking of the staff saved several lives. On hearing the gunshots and the commotion, the nurses had shifted all the patients and had locked all the doors before Kasab and Ismail could reach them. Unable to get past the iron grill doors, the duo left. They tried to find a car they could hijack and fired at some other cars. Finally they sped off to Malabar Hill. On the run and unsure of the roads in Mumbai, Kasab had no clue which way they were going and what was their next objective. They only knew that they had to cause maximum damage. On the way they came across a barricade at Vinoli Chowpatty. Initially they were not sure whether they would be able to cross it and they stopped a little way off. They then decided to try to drive through the low divider and failed. The police immediately ambushed them and they were overpowered in the gun battle. Both of them were taken to the hospital where Ismail succumbed to his injuries, and Kasab was taken under custody.

During this entire operation, there was confusion all across. From outside the buildings that the terrorists had taken over, the police and other security agencies could see and hear the fire and the gun shots. Several specialized forces like the National Security Guard were brought in to tackle the situation. However, the task of the security agencies was made tougher by the media.

In an attempt to provide 'live coverage', television channels provided their viewers the latest updates and videos of the locations, which actually helped the terrorists inside. While the policemen and security agencies had no idea about the location of the terrorists inside, the members of Lashkar-e-Taiba, sitting in Pakistan, were glued to Indian news channels which relayed the movements of the security agencies. The terrorist organization passed on the information to the terrorists inside the buildings.

The Supreme Court later addressed the irresponsibility of the media in aiding the terrorists through their 'second to second' reporting. It stated[30]:

'The reckless coverage of the terrorist attack by the channels thus gave rise to a situation where on the one hand the t~~errorist~~ were completely hidden from the security forces [...] and on the other hand the positions of the security forces, their weapons

---

[30]*Mohammed Ajmal Mohammad Amir Kasab @ Abu Mujahid vs. State of Maharashtra*, [2012] 8 S.C.R 295.

and all their operational movements were being watched by the collaborators across the border on TV screens and being communicated to the terrorists [...] But it is beyond doubt that the way their operations were freely shown made the task of the security forces not only exceedingly difficult but also dangerous and risky [...]'.

TRIAL

The attack began on 26 November 2008 at about 9.15 p.m. and it ended when the last of the attackers, who was holed up in the Taj, was killed by Indian security forces at around 9.00 a.m. on 29 November 2008. The terrorists killed about 166 people and injured, often grievously, 238.

The entire incident had been a three-day nightmare for Indians. Thousands of people had either suffered personal losses or knew close friends or family members who had been affected. There was a strong public drive for decisive action. It would emerge later that India and Pakistan were at the brink of war at this time, the animosity having risen to its highest since the Kargil war. The US and other international powers were concerned and kept a close watch on the situation.

Kasab was put in judicial custody to await trial. Popular sentiment was against him. People felt that there was no need for a trial. Kasab had been caught red-handed and pictures of him with the gun featured on every front page. Many demanded that Kasab should be hanged. Nobody wanted to wait for years to see a man who had ruthlessly destroyed hundreds of families spend taxpayers' money sitting in jail. Everyone had had enough.

However, the Constitution of India mandates that no person can be deprived of his right to life and personal liberty without following the procedure established by law. Article 14 of the Constitution guarantees everyone a right to a fair hearing. Therefore, like every other case, procedure was followed. Even though no advocate was willing to take Kasab's case, eventually a lawyer was appointed, and the case was admitted. Kasab too got a chance to redeem himself, justify his actions, and present his side of the story. Even though the public wanted him to be hanged without a trial, it was shown that the fabric of justice in India will not be altered, even when dealing with a terrorist.

A special court was established to hear the matter, and the prosecution meticulously prepared a complaint hundreds of pages long. Photographs, medical and forensic reports, CCTV recordings, phone call records, station diary entries, police logs and records of damage to property were presented as proof of the crime in front of the judges. Testimonies of witnesses revealed tales of those who had encountered the terrorists and survived, and others whose lives had been shattered through the acts of the accused.

Kasab volunteered a confession, which exposed the entire planning process and which incriminated him. His pleas during his trial were colourful, to say the least. He took the juvenile plea thereby suggesting that he cannot be tried as an adult as he is below the required age. It was, however, determined by the sessions court by conducting an ossification test that Kasab was more than twenty years old and an adult as per law. Kasab also claimed denial of due process and fair trial, and claimed that half the terrorists were of Indian origin. His lawyer even sought to retract his confession, but in vain. Kasab's behaviour during the trial was no less interesting. He took it upon himself to entertain the media. He would laugh and joke with them. Far from displaying any remorse, he appeared to find the court proceedings amusing, to the point where Justice Tahiliani had to direct him to 'remain serious in court'. He came to court with cotton in his ears as he didn't want to hear the prosecutor's voice. Kasab threw tantrums and refused jail food on more than one occasion—he threw the utensils and cheekily asked for mutton biryani. These antics earned him much public wrath in India.

He was eventually found guilty of waging war against the nation, criminal conspiracy, murder and terror-related provisions under the Unlawful Activities (Prevention) Act, 1967. Being charged with conspiracy meant that Kasab was not only held guilty for the innocents that he and Ismail had killed, but also for all the people who had lost their lives at the hands of the other eight terrorists they had conspired with.

Kasab went on to appeal in the High Court, and then in the Supreme Court where his death sentence was upheld. In confirming the death penalty the courts stated that:

'[...] The conspiracy was to launch a murderous attack on Mumbai regarding it as the financial centre of the country; to kill as many Indians and foreign nationals as possible; to take Indians and foreign nationals as hostages for using them as bargaining chips in regard to the terrorists' demands; and to try to incite communal strife and insurgency; all with the intent to weaken the country from within [...] In terms of loss of life and property, and more importantly in its traumatizing effect, this case stands alone, or it is at least the very rarest of rare to come before this Court since the birth of the Republic. Therefore, it should also attract the rarest of rare punishment...'[31].

The only mitigating factor in this case was Kasab's youth,

---

[31]*Mohammed Ajmal Mohammad Amir Kasab vs. Abu Mujahid vs. State of Maharashtra*, [2012] 8 S.C.R 295.

as Kasab was only twenty-two years old at the time. The court stated that this was not enough to mitigate the sentence, and as no remorse had been shown, it was unlikely that reform was possible. Kasab filed a mercy petition to the president as a last-ditch effort to save his life, but it was turned down.

Kasab was hanged on 21 November 2012 at 7.30 a.m. and buried at the Yerwada Jail in Pune.

AUTHORS' NOTE

This episode tested the credibility of the judiciary and the media in India. The Kasab case was probably one of the swiftest in the history of the Indian judiciary, and unlike some other convicts on death row, Kasab did not have to wait for years for his final day.

In a case so emotionally charged as this one, where even lawyers hesitated to represent Kasab, every rule of law was followed, and justice was served in the end. Although no sympathy was lost on Kasab, he was well represented by his lawyers, and was given a fighting chance under the law, whether he deserved it or not. It is important to show the enemies of the country that even though they tried to destroy India and bring down one of the world's greatest and most vibrant democracies, India and Indians as a collective stood tall as a nation, and not even the worst terrorist attack could make them forget their principles of justice.

On the other hand, the Indian government also sent across a message to the international community that even the worst offender would not be punished without due process of law. This would help India in the long run to extradite criminals from other countries. This also put Pakistan in a difficult position, having to face international pressure to cooperate with India on the investigation on one side, and having to neutralize the high tension within the country on the other. In the end, Pakistan refused to accept Kasab's body, calling him a 'non-state actor', in spite of him being a Pakistani national, and India gave him a proper burial after his death.

While the judiciary lived up to its role in this case, the behaviour of the media was criticized. It sensationalized the incident in a chilling, horrific manner, and the minute-by-minute telecast of the terrorist attack put the lives of the hostages and the security forces in danger. Several questions were raised—did the media channels act unethically just to secure an audience? Had their actions put the lives of Indians in jeopardy? Can freedom of speech be stretched to such an extent that it puts lives at risk? The media needs to introspect and take a more responsible role during such testing times.

THE NITISH KATARA MURDER

*'A special legislation (for honour killing) will certainly be
a welcome effort as it will help in generating additional
protection to the victims.'*

—Justice P. Sathasivam, on 29 June 2013[32]

BACKGROUND

Nitish Katara and Bharti Yadav, batchmates turned lovers,
attended a wedding together on 16-17 February 2002 in
Ghaziabad, where Bharti's mother, her brothers Vikas and Vishal,
and her sister Bhavna, were also present. On the night of 17
February 2002, Nitish accompanied Vikas and Vishal into their
SUV. The next morning, his body was found, hammered to death
and set aflame using petrol. The love story had gone horribly
wrong, ending in an honour killing.

Nitish Katara was twenty-four years old when he was
murdered. He was a graduate of the Institute of Management
Technology, Ghaziabad (IMT-G), and was working in Delhi. He
was the son of an officer in the Indian Administrative Services.
While studying at IMT-G, he met fellow classmate Bharti. Their
acquaintance turned into friendship and soon enough, romance

---

[32]'Special law will deter honour killings, says Sathasivam', *The Hindu* (New
Delhi, 30 June 2013).

blossomed between the two. When Bharti's family found out about it, they strongly disapproved of the relationship, though no specific reason was found for their opposition. Nitish was also threatened several times with dire consequences if he did not leave Bharti. Nitish, an idealist, firmly believed that what was happening was an injustice and felt that he should stand up to it. The Yadavs were a highly influential political family in the area, and Bharti's father, D.P. Yadav was a major politician with criminal cases pending against him.

On the night in question, the two of them had attended the wedding of a friend. Photographs showed the presence of Bharti's brothers at the wedding. Four witnesses said that they had seen Vikas and Vishal leading Nitish into their Tata Safari. That was the last time Nitish was seen alive. His friend Diwakar, who had accompanied Nitish to the wedding, attempted to find Nitish and at around 3.00 a.m., knocked on the Kataras' door. Bharti, who had also been worried about Nitish's whereabouts, used her sister's mobile phone to try to reach Nitish all night long. When Neelam, Nitish's mother, called Bharti, she became worried that her brothers were possibly the reason behind Nitish's disappearance. She advised Neelam to call the police. A first information report was filed and warrants were issued at 11.00 a.m. the next morning, based on the statements of Bharti and Neelam. Nitish Katara's body was found badly beaten and burnt. It was a gruesome sight to behold. The damage was so intense that his entrails were exposed.

CONFESSIONS

After the warrants were issued, the Yadav brothers were arrested by the Uttar Pradesh police and were taken in for questioning.

This started off a sensational legal drama that grabbed the nation's attention. Under Indian law, a confession is admissible in court only if it is recorded in the presence of a magistrate. This law exists to check the abuse of police power. The Yadav brothers confessed to the police that they had kidnapped and murdered Nitish Katara. The Uttar Pradesh police recorded their confessions on an audiotape. The confessions were deemed inadmissible as evidence in a court of law as they had not been recorded in the presence of a magistrate as required by law. All hell broke loose when the confession tape was leaked to a major private news channel in India. The entire country heard Vikas Yadav confessing to the kidnap and murder of Nitish Katara.

To an average person in India, this confession was acceptable proof of the Yadav brothers' guilt. However, it was not so easy for the courts to reach a similar conclusion. The rule of law requires that a trial be conducted where all the evidence is considered and both the prosecution and the accused are given an opportunity to present their case. If there is a crime, no matter how convinced the general public may be about guilt of the accused person, it is only after a trial and a conviction that he may be punished.

TRIAL

Crucial to this case was establishing motive. There were no eyewitnesses to the crime, so circumstantial evidence had to be relied upon. The prosecution had to prove that Bharti Yadav and Nitish Katara had been in a relationship. In order to do this, Bharti's testimony was vital. She had made statements to the police earlier, ranging from saying that she loved Nitish 'with her heart' to saying that they were just good friends.[33] During the course of the trial, Bharti had left for the United Kingdom for further studies and was working as a staff nurse at a local hospital there. For two years the prosecution attempted to obtain her testimony but to no avail. Even after numerous summons and non-bailable warrants were issued, Bharti refused to testify.

The Uttar Pradesh state prosecution submitted to the court that she had to be dropped as a witness in order to move the trial to its close. However, Nitish's mother Neelam challenged this in the Supreme Court. She claimed that this action was in bad faith and had been proposed under the influence of political pressure. She also sought the location of the trial be changed in order to ensure the smooth delivery of justice.

A CHANGE IN VENUE

In India, a crime is tried by the first court that takes cognizance of the crime. This is usually in the territory where the crime occurred. However, the Supreme Court may, in select cases, if it sees fit, change the location of the trial in order to ensure that it goes through smoothly. This is done especially if there is any apprehension that a particular court may not be able to pass an independent and unbiased verdict. This is done to preserve the fairness and impartiality of the system.

The Supreme Court, in this case, agreed with Nitish's mother and held that the Yadavs, being sons of a member of parliament, could exert influence over the administration of justice in the area, and therefore, ordered that the trial be moved from Uttar

[33]'Nitish was a close friend: Bharti', *The Telegraph* (New Delhi, 2 December 2006).

Pradesh to the courts in Delhi.

In 2006, the Ministry of External Affairs revoked Bharti's passport and her visa to remain in the UK was soon to expire. She was in danger of being declared a proclaimed offender, and so had to return to testify. Her testimony was captured on camera. Members of the public were not permitted to view it, however, the defendants' family members were allowed to be present in court.

THE TESTIMONY

After intense cross-examination by the prosecution, Bharti denied that an affair had ever occurred between her and Nitish and claimed that they were mere friends. However, there were evidence on record—cards and gifts that she had sent to Nitish. The prosecution used this to establish the existence of an affair between Nitish and Bharti, thereby establishing motive.

Other evidence, such as a watch and the murder weapon recovered from the scene of the crime, allowed the prosecution to establish circumstantial evidence against the accused. However, the case was further complicated when three of the four witnesses who saw the Yadavs take Nitish into the car changed or modified their testimony.

A key witness, Ajay Kumar (sometimes referred to as Ajay Katara, though he was not related to Nitish Katara or his family), also filed a complaint with the court saying that he was being threatened to change his testimony. An attempt at poisoning him was also reported to the police. Finally, under police protection, he testified in the case.

The court in 2008 finally convicted Vikas and Vishal Yadav of kidnapping, conspiracy and murder and described the crime as an honour killing. They were sentenced to life imprisonment, even though the prosecution had asked for the death penalty. They were also fined ₹1,60,000 each. They were to serve their sentences in Tihar Jail.

Sukhdev Pehalwan, a contract killer, was also convicted for the same offence in the year 2011. An appeal was filed by Nitish's mother, the convicts as well as the prosecution. On 2 April 2014, the High Court upheld the three convictions. The pleas of the State and the victim's mother, Neelam Katara, for death sentences against the convicts is still pending.[34]

AUTHORS' NOTE

It has been revealed in news reports that Vikas Yadav has been granted bail sixty-six times since his conviction, details of which are not readily available. The law provides that the state government may allow the parole or probation of an offender as a matter of discretion. These bail applications were granted for various reasons, ranging from having to attend a wedding to numerous trips to the hospital.

The case highlights several points. It shows that if the media plays an active but non-intrusive role in pursuing a case, it helps the victim or his family receive justice. It also brings to light how politicians can influence criminal trials if they choose to do so. The Indian judicial system, though often criticized for being slow and corrupt, proved that justice is delivered in the end in spite of the best efforts of the powerful accused persons to manipulate the system.

---

[34]'Nitish Katara's murder honour killing, warrants death penalty, HC told', *Deccan Herald* (New Delhi, 11 July 2014).

This case also highlights the need to tackle the menace of 'honour killing', which continues to plague Indian society along with other issues such as patriarchy, caste, communal tension and an ever-widening economic divide. In all fairness to the Indian media, they are working with zeal to fight this barbaric practice and spread awareness among the masses.

P.V. NARASIMHA RAO:
THE TAINTED CHANAKYA

*'Corruption is like a ball of snow, one it's set a rolling it must
increase.'*

—Charles Caleb Colton

THE 1991 ELECTIONS were conducted against the backdrop of
the Mandal Commission report—which ensured 27 per cent
reservation for OBCs in government jobs—and the Babri Masjid
issue in Ayodhya. A day after the first round of polling took
place, Rajiv Gandhi was assassinated while campaigning in Tamil
Nadu. Though the Indian National Congress had done poorly
in the first round of polls, it came back stronger after Gandhi's
assassination. The final verdict was a hung parliament, with the
Congress emerging as the single largest party. P.V. Narasimha
Rao was invited by the president, R. Venkataraman, to form a
government; he took the oath as the tenth Prime Minister of
India. Earlier in 1991, Rao had asked Rajiv Gandhi permission
to retire from active politics. A distinguished poet, Rao wished
to spend his twilight years composing music and writing poems
in his home state of Andhra Pradesh. The assassination of Rajiv
Gandhi and the leadership crisis in the Congress meant that Rao
had to step in and hold the reins of the party.

1991: THE CRISIS

The rigid nationalized economy of India had led to the 'Licence Raj' by the 1980s—the growth of new businesses was constricted by bureaucracy and red tape. India had balance-of-payments problems, putting it in massive debt, which lead to a full-blown economic crisis by the beginning of the 1990s. The rupee was at a fixed peg back then and this led to over-valuation of the rupee. This, along with other economic factors, like the current account deficit and a dearth of investor confidence after the assassination of Rajiv Gandhi, left India with little investment and a depleting reserve of foreign exchange. The balance-of-payments crisis had spilled over to an external trade crisis and India was at the brink of a financial Armageddon. It did not help that there was a minority government at the centre that had to take charge of this crisis. Horse trading with allies had ensured that the government could at least gain a simple majority in the lower house of parliament, allowing it to pass the budget and create some semblance of stability amidst a storm.

Narasimha Rao shocked everyone by inducting Dr Manmohan Singh, the ex-governor of the RBI and the ex-deputy chairman of the Planning Commission, into his cabinet as the new finance minister. A technocrat and academician, Dr Singh was thrown into the deep end during one of the most difficult financial scenarios India had ever witnessed. Over the first few months of the Narasimha Rao government, the International Monetary Fund (IMF) was called in to bail India out. Gold reserves were flown by army choppers to the IMF to act as collateral for loans to cover the balance of payments. The IMF bailout came with certain structural reform conditions, which India had to accept and adhere to. These conditions, along with the reform policies of Manmohan Singh, and with the support of Narasimha Rao, lead to the liberalization of the Indian economy. The economic reforms of 1991 sounded the end of the License Raj. Industrial licencing requirements were removed almost overnight and the capital markets were opened up for foreign participation. Foreign direct investment was introduced and thus the recovery of the Indian economy was initiated. Though, in hindsight, this reform played a vital role in establishing India as an emerging economic power a decade later, these reforms were not introduced without opposition. Rao's coalition could only survive with the support of the Left and by 1993, he was forced to face a vote of no confidence on the floor of the house.

NO CONFIDENCE IN RAO

Ajay Mukhopadhyay of the Communist Party of India (Marxist) pushed for a no-confidence motion in 1993, putting the fate of the government at stake. On party lines, the Congress was short of fourteen votes to gain a majority in the lower house. The motion was taken up for discussion by the house and was put to vote on 20 July 1993. The Congress government survived the trust vote by exactly fourteen votes and thus became the first minority government in the history of independent India to complete a full five-year term.

A scandal broke soon after the Narasimha Rao government completed its term in 1996—Ravindra Kumar of Rashtriya Mukti Morcha filed a complaint with the CBI saying that during the trust vote in 1993, cash bribes to the tune of ₹3 crore had been paid to members of parliament from the Jharkhand Mukti Morcha and other parties to ensure that the no-confidence motion was defeated on the floor of the house. News of this scandal sent ripples across the country and through political establishments. While allegations of corruption were common with politicians and the bureaucracy, the bribing of members of parliament for votes meant that politics had hit a new low.

A QUESTION OF PRIVILEGE

The parliament of India acknowledges and incorporates many of the traditions of the parliament of the United Kingdom of Great Britain and Northern Ireland. One such tradition is that of parliamentary privilege. This concept of parliamentary privilege goes as far back as 1689 and states that members of the parliament shall have immunity for all acts done while on the floor of the house. This essentially means that no court may call into question any act, statement or vote by a member of parliament. Any infraction or breach by a member is to be dealt with by the parliament itself. Each of the two houses of the Indian parliament, i.e., the Lok Sabha and the Rajya Sabha, has a committee on privileges which deals with infractions committed while on the floor of the house. The parliament takes privilege very seriously and the Constitution of India protects this right explicitly. Parliamentary privilege was the first defence asserted when Narasimha Rao was accused of bribery during the no-confidence vote. This was challenged and the applicability of the parliamentary privilege defence in this case was questioned in the Supreme Court. The Supreme Court of India, being the keeper and interpreter of the Constitution, had to decide if the prosecution of Narasimha Rao and others could go on.

Narasimha Rao claimed that since the allegations were with respect to a vote in the parliament, privilege should prevail and the prosecution be deemed unconstitutional. His claim was founded on the reasoning that the members of the parliament require such a privilege in order to exercise their duties effectively and that it should be widely construed in order to include matters even connected with the business of the house. In relation to applicability of certain other statutes, Narasimha Rao further argued that a member of parliament was not a 'public servant' and therefore could not be prosecuted under anti-corruption laws like the Prevention of Corruption Act, 1986. He reasoned that since members of parliament performed a constitutional function, they could not be regarded as public servants.

The Supreme Court, however, did not agree with these arguments. The court said that allowing privilege to be invoked as a means to prevent a member from being prosecuted for corruption would undermine the rule of law. When a member of parliament is prosecuted for bribery, parliamentary privilege should not be invoked as a defence. The court further stated that privilege could only apply to a vote or a speech made in the parliament. If the bribe had been given before the voting, it constituted an offence in itself and could be prosecuted in the courts. Hence, the Supreme Court ruled that Narasimha Rao could not invoke privilege as a defence in this case. It further held that a member of parliament, by virtue of the fact that he exercises a public duty, is a public servant for the purposes of anti-corruption laws and therefore can be prosecuted for offences under such laws.[35] This intervention paved the way for the first ever trial of a former Prime Minster for corruption.

---

[35]*P.V. Narasimha Rao vs. State*, AIR 1998 SC 2120.

CONVICTION AND FALL

After being granted bail by the special CBI court in 1996, Rao became a political nobody, achieving infamy again in 2000 when the trial court convicted Rao of corruption for bribing members of parliament. However, in 2002, the Delhi High Court overturned this conviction, as the statements of the key witnesses in the case were found to be contradictory and conflicting. Rao was acquitted for lack of evidence.

In Scotland, under the Scots Law, criminal courts have a principle where they may return not two but three verdicts. Along with the usual verdicts of 'guilty' or 'not guilty', the Scottish criminal courts could return the verdict of 'not proven' for lack of evidence. Perhaps the Delhi High Court's judgment exonerating Rao could be best perceived as a verdict of 'not proven'. Suspicions still loomed and there was no coming back for Narasimha Rao politically. Even in the Congress, in light of this scandal and the return of the Gandhi family in the form of Sonia Gandhi and then Rahul Gandhi, Narasimha Rao became a forgotten man.

AUTHORS' NOTE

The greatest legacy of Narasimha Rao would probably be the role he had played in initiating the liberalization of the Indian economy. And the greatest legacy of the Narsimha Rao case will be that it had highlighted the rule of law and democracy in India. The world's largest democracy put a former Prime Minister on trial for corruption. Even though he was not convicted due to lack of evidence, it reaffirmed the belief that in a democracy, the law is supreme and no one is above it. While a series of scams and corruption scandals are emerging today in India, it has to be seen whether the high and mighty accused in such cases are brought to justice, or whether they are also acquitted on the basis of insufficient evidence.

HARSHAD MEHTA: THE BIG BULL

'It's not a question of enough, pal. It's a zero sum game, somebody wins, somebody loses. Money itself isn't lost or made, it's simply transferred from one perception to another.'

—Gordon Gekko, in the movie *Wall Street*

THE FORT AREA of Mumbai is the heart of the financial capital of India. The name is derived from Fort George that the East India Company built in the eighteenth century around the Bombay Castle. It would not be wrong to say that the financial health of India is dependent on this area. It is home to the Reserve Bank of India, the Bombay Stock Exchange, the headquarters of the State Bank of India and other important financial organizations. The old-world commercial buildings here rank amongst some of the most expensive real estate in the world. Like the borough of the City of London within greater London, this is also a city within a city, a world in itself.

The people who work here, from the big players in their imported cars, to the ordinary mortals streaming out of the train stations, exist in equilibrium within this city. However, even before the Mumbai blasts of 1993, there was another explosion, albeit metaphorically, that ripped through the financial capital of India. On 23 April 1992, the people of India opened the *Times of India* and read about a scam so big that it sent shockwaves all the way to the Prime Minister's office. The question was, who was Harshad Mehta and how did this son of a small businessman from Gujarat bring the entire financial system to its knees? The story smelled of 'regulatory failure' and a failure in understanding how business in the financial heart of the country works.

The government had recently liberalized the Indian economy. The years of the Licence Raj were finally at an end. Those in the capital market community celebrated, saying that it was finally legal to make money in India. The stock markets reacted with joy and thus began the great Bull Run at the Bombay Stock Exchange (BSE). But who was actually behind this Bull Run? Where was the money coming from? The Harshad Mehta scam shook the very foundations of the financial industry in India and continues to hold a place in the imagination of many.

THE RISE

Harshad Mehta was the son of a middle-class businessman from Rajkot, Gujarat. He spent most of his early life in the suburbs of Kandivali, Mumbai, and then in Raipur, where his family moved. After being expelled from school, he passed the board examinations as a private candidate. He studied commerce at the Lala Lajpat Rai College, Mumbai, and then took up a job at the New India Assurance Company. However, he was not content with the prospect of a middle-class life. He craved more and set off to join the stock markets, becoming a 'jobber'—a person who acts on behalf of the broker on the floor of the exchange—at the BSE in the early 1980s. At the time, the BSE was very different from its highly efficient computerized version today. It was akin to a grand bazaar with people shouting prices in loud voices and transactions being conducted across the floor. Harshad later became a sub-broker. Over the course of the 1980s, he and his brother, Ashwin, managed to become members of the BSE and founded their own firm, Growmore Investments.[36]

The stock market was Harshad's world. He quick grasped the secrets of the trade and had great foresight, ensuring he quickly climbed the ladder of success. He drove a Lexus in a nation that was still getting used to the idea of the Maruti 800, he lived in a posh terrace flat with its own game room and private mini-theatre in a prime area of Mumbai. He wore expensive double-breasted suits and wined and dined in the most elite restaurants and bars in the city. At this time, Harshad was also becoming a familiar name with the banks that control India's financial destiny and the average Indian investor started looking up to him for cues on what to do. He earned the nickname Big Bull because of his optimistic position on the Indian stock markets.[37]

It would probably be pertinent to pause Harshad's story here for a moment and understand, very simply, how the capital markets work and how stocks are priced.

The markets work on the most primitive of human instincts—the herd mentality. The leader of the herd sets the path and everyone else follows. This can be applied to stock prices as well. The shares of a company are limited in number. So the owner of the shares will sell them to the highest bidder to get the best price for them. To do so, the seller and the buyer have to negotiate prices. If there is more demand than supply, the price of the share will go up, since the buyers will compete

---

[36]Sucheta Dalal, Debashis Basu, *The Scam: From Harshad Metha to Ketan Parekh*. India: Kensource Business Books, 2009.
[37]'"Big Bull" Harshad Mehta Dead', *The Hindu Business Line* (Mumbai, 1 January 2002).

and raise the price for the limited number of shares available.

This is when the herd mentality comes into play—people look for cues and signals to guide them in their purchasing decisions as most of them lack the financial knowledge to forecast share prices. So when the Big Bull says that he is buying the shares of company X at a certain price, everyone who takes their cues from the Big Bull will start to place orders for X. This will inevitably push the price of company X's shares up.

Information is key, and when the common man was taking his first venture into the equity markets in the early 1990s, there was very little information available. So players like Harshad Mehta were able to influence investor decisions and thereby push up the price of the stocks. It is like blowing air into a bubble—the bubble gets bigger and bigger until it bursts, and there is nothing left but air. This is exactly what happened with the stock price bubble in the early 1990s. Harshad Mehta and others convinced investors to pull their money out of banks and put it in the equity markets, and that too on specific stocks that they had picked. When financial analysts pointed out that such a steep rise in stock prices is not good for the market, they used such jargon-filled explanations that investor confidence remained intact and the great bull run continued. When the Big Bull ceased to roar, the bubble burst. Many investors lost their entire life savings. However, this was only part of the story—the mechanism by which Harshad Mehta and others like him had engineered a bull run. The scam, which Harshad masterminded, was much more sinister and involved a lot of public money.[38]

---

[38] Sucheta Dalal, Debashis Basu, *The Scam: From Harshad Metha to Ketan Parekh*. India: Kensource Business Books, 2009.

THE SCAM EXPLAINED

The RBI mandates that all commercial banks should maintain a certain percent of their deposits in gold or government bonds and securities before extending credit (Statutory Liquidity Ratio or SLR). This was done so that the government could finance its spending and control bank credit. The banks would have to show their books to the RBI every week to prove that they had maintained their SLRs. The rule was simple—at the end of the week, the bank was required to have securities higher than its SLR; during the week it just had to maintain it. Government debt, while secure, provides one with a very meagre interest rate compared to the debt market. Many banks began selling government debt on the market during the week, and then bought it back one day before they had to submit their books to the RBI. This way, they had more funds to lend in the money market and make a profit. But how do these banks who sell government securities meet the banks who buy them? This is where brokers like Harshad came in. They brokered these securities deals between banks, and by doing so, they made a hefty commission. In addition, they carried a large amount of capital for a short period of time, which they invested in the stock market and made huge profits.[39]

Harshad dealt with a large number of banks, so when he took the securities he did not know who the eventual buyer would be, and vice versa. He encouraged the banks to write cheques directly to him. This was technically illegal. Harshad used this system to squeeze money out of the banking system and pump

---

[39]'What Harshad Mehta Did – The Stock Scam', *The Bull Rider* (February 2010).

it into the capital markets. Banks were not allowed to invest in the capital markets. Harshad also made use of bank receipts (BR). Instead of selling the securities directly, most banks used to issue BRs. The BRs could be used as proof of sale of a security. Harshad found the Bank of Karad (BOK) and the Metropolitan Co-operative Bank (MCB) to be friendly banks who were willing to issue fake BRs for a fee. Harshad used these BRs as proof to convince banks to trade with him.

This scam was used to manipulate the system and brokers like Harshad made more money than legitimate investors and stockbrokers. When the SBI demanded payment overnight in order to reconcile their balance sheet, Harshad was unable to pay up. This lead to panic in SBI, and rumours eventually leaked to the press.[40]

The *Times of India* ran a front-page article about a certain broker who had been asked to pay ₹500 crore to the SBI on 23 April 1992. By the time the story broke, Harshad had paid off most of that amount, and he later paid it back in full. He managed to get the National Housing Bank (NHB) (a fully owned subsidiary of the RBI) to give him the money, which he deposited in his ANZ Grindlay's bank account and which he used to pay SBI. At this point, the RBI began noticing anomalies. When it discovered the scam, and the fact that its own subsidiary had been involved in bailing out Harshad, it began hunting down the culprit. The RBI ordered the SBI and Grindlay's to return the money to the NHB and sought to recover the rest of Harshad's illegal money from other sources. The SBI complied under the pain of a finance ministry directive while Grindlay's managed

---

[40]Sucheta Dalal, Debashis Basu, *The Scam: From Harshad Metha to Ketan Parekh*. India: Kensource Business Books, 2009.

to get away. The entire financial system was under scrutiny and someone had to pay.[41]

THE SCRAMBLE FOR A CULPRIT

Overnight the nation woke up to the size and the scale of this scam. Many did not understand what had happened and the repercussions. Questions were raised in parliament and the government had to respond. The CBI was called in to investigate. At the same time, the RBI began looking into the books of bank officials and the income tax department started enquiring if Harshad had paid the exchequer its dues. The government also stepped in by forming a Joint Parliamentary Committee (JPC) to investigate the scandal. With great fanfare, it was announced that a special court would be formed to try these offenders speedily. The investigation quickly turned into an administrative blame game. The RBI sought to protect its reputation and tried to protect the NHB and cover up its own regulatory failures. The JPC attempted to find fault with the government. Reforms were introduced in the February 1992 budget, but they did not find wide acceptance amongst a majority of the middle class. The government found itself on a sticky wicket. If it did not act now, the media would realize that the scam was due to regulatory failure and would link it to the recent reforms. The bears returned to Dalal Street and overnight, many of the bulls exited their positions. The market tanked and many ordinary investors lost their life savings. However, a man had to be held guilty and for that, a crime had to be proved. Harshad's fate now rested on the

---

[41]Sucheta Dalal, Debashis Basu, *The Scam: From Harshad Metha to Ketan Parekh*. India: Kensource Business Books, 2009.

CBI investigation and the outcome of his trial.[42]

THE TRIAL

Harshad hired the country's top lawyers to defend him, namely Ram Jethmalani and his son, Mahesh. Ram Jethmalani was not new to highly public trials—he was, and still is, a veteran in that field. The special court provided for a custodian to be appointed by the country to handle and dispose the assets of the accused if found guilty. The custodian was also given the power to declare certain securities as being tainted as they had passed through the accused before reaching their present holders. The securities were largely shares in major companies on the BSE and were, at that point, held by the aam aadmi (common man). The new holders of the shares could not dispose the securities without getting a no-objection certificate from the court. This required countless affidavits and other documents and many just gave up on the process. Of the several cases filed against him, Harshad was only convicted in one case—the Maruit Udyog case—and he was sentenced to five years of rigorous imprisonment and a fine of ₹25,000.[43]

THE MARUTI UDYOG CASE

The case concerned the forgery of BRs and the direct deposit of cash into Harshad's bank account at ANZ Grindlay's. Harshad

---

[42]Sucheta Dalal, Debashis Basu, *The Scam: From Harshad Metha to Ketan Parekh*. India: Kensource Business Books, 2009.

[43]'Harshad Mehta sentenced to five years' RI,' *Rediff* (Mumbai, 28 September 1999).

appeared as Accused No. 5 in the prosecution charge sheet and was charged with criminal misappropriation of property under Section 403 of the IPC along with being party to a criminal conspiracy under Section 120-A of the Indian Penal Code.[44] There were four others accused in the case, which primarily involved the sale and purchase of Unit Trust of India (UTI) securities by Maruti Udyog Limited (MUL) and Harshad Mehta. MUL purchased securities from UCO Bank and agreed to a reversal of the transaction a month later. Harshad brokered the transaction and routed the money through his own accounts in Bank of America and ANZ Grindlay's Bank. MUL directly deposited the money into Harshad's account and then received payment from the same account. Documents were forged in order to make the transaction look legitimate to the board of MUL. Further, Harshad also engaged in four other shorter transactions with MUL, which he claimed were loans against BRs as security.

When the case went on appeal to the Supreme Court, the accused was represented by Ram Jethmalani, and the prosecution was represented by the Solicitor General of India at that time, Harish Salve. The Supreme Court bench consisted of Justice M. Shah, Justice B. Agarwal and Justice A. Pasayat. Justice B. Agarwal and Justice A. Pasayat wrote the majority opinion dismissing the appeals while Justice M. Shah allowed for the appeals, stating that the prosecution failed to make its case and there was no *prima facie* illegality in the MUL transactions.

It is interesting to examine the reasoning that Justice A. Pasayat used to uphold the conviction of Harshad. Quoting from

---

[44]Para 125, *Ram Narain Poply and Ors. vs. Central Bureau of Investigation*, AIR 2003 SC 7748.

an earlier judgment of the Supreme Court he stated:

'The cause of the community deserves better treatment at the hands of the Court in the discharge of its judicial functions. The Community or the State is not a persona non grata whose cause may be treated with disdain. The entire community is aggrieved if economic offenders who ruin the economy of the State are not brought to book. A murder may be committed in the heat of moment upon passions being aroused. An economic offence is committed with cool calculation and deliberate design with an eye on personal profit regardless of the consequence to the Community. A disregard for the interest of the Community can be manifested only at the cost of forfeiting the trust and faith of the Community in the system to administer justice in an even-handed manner without fear of criticism from the quarters which view white-collar crimes with a permissive eye, unmindful of the damage done to the National Economy and National Interest.'[45]

He further states, 'Unfortunately in the last few years, the country has seen an alarming rise in white-collar crimes which has affected the fibre of the country's economic structure. These cases are nothing but private gain at the cost of public, and lead to economic disaster.'[46]

Justice M. Shah, in his dissenting opinion, was vocal in his discontent with the way the prosecution of the case had been carried out. He stated that Harshad had made a declaration that he had bribed the then Prime Minister, Narasimha Rao, and

---

[45]Para 102, *Ram Narain Poply and Ors. vs. Central Bureau of Investigation*, AIR 2003 SC 7748.

[46]Para 103, *Ram Narain Poply and Ors. vs. Central Bureau of Investigation*, AIR 2003 SC 7748.

the investigation was being carried out in order to ensure that the witness to that transaction stays on the prosecution side in exchange for a full pardon.[47]

However, in the early hours of 31 December 2001, Harshad passed away at the Thane Prison Hospital due to a heart ailment, leaving behind his wife, Jyoti, and their two sons.[48]

The judgment clearly shows that there was a divided opinion at the time as to whether Harshad's actions actually constituted an offence and warranted criminal investigation. The other investigations before the special court are still pending. When Harshad died, there were over twenty-eight cases pending before various courts in the country. Only the Maruti Udyog case was completed during Harshad's lifetime.[49] A special court constituted under The Special Court Act, 1992, in Special Case No. 1 of 1993 had convicted nine persons for criminal conspiracy and criminal breach of trust. An appeal was filed against the same by the accused persons.

The Supreme Court, in its decision on 7 August 2009,[50] upheld the conviction of four persons for the offenses of criminal conspiracy and criminal breach of trust. S.V. Ramathan was acquitted by the court and the court did not interfere with the convictions of the remaining three persons for the same offenses. The persons convicted included the then chairman of

---

[47]Para 141, *Ram Narain Poply and Ors. vs. Central Bureau of Investigation*, AIR 2003 SC 7748.

[48]'Big Bull' Harshad Mehta Dead,' *The Hindu Business Line* (Mumbai, 1 January 2002).

[49]Ibid.

[50]*R. Venkatakrishnan vs. Central Bureau of Investigation*, Cr. Appeal No. 76 of 2004.

UCO Bank; the general manager of UCO Bank; the manager of the bank's Mumbai branch[51]; the assistant general manager of NHB; and the assistant vice-president of Growmore Research and Assets Management Ltd, which had represented Harshad Mehta in undertaking security transactions.

Each of the convicts received different punishments, i.e., rigorous imprisonment for varied periods and fines of different amounts were imposed upon each of them. The court also laid down a sentence for simple imprisonment for each of them in case any of them default in paying the fine imposed.[52]

AFTER THE SCAM

After the scam, a great need was felt for proper market-conducive regulation and the Securities Exchange Board of India (SEBI) was finally given statutory powers to regulate the Indian financial markets. The RBI also had to change its regulation policy entirely. Harshad's prediction that the reforms would take the Indian capital market sky high did prove to be true—the Sensex rose from 3,000-odd points in 1992 to well over 13,000 levels in the first decade of the twentieth century.

Many of the cases against Harshad Mehta, both civil and criminal, are still pending and the special court continues to conduct regular hearings against all those involved in the scam. His property is still under dispute and banks are still trying to

---

[51]The UCO Bank had loaned a sum of ₹40 crore to Harshad, which was 'call money' it had obtained from the NHB? The money had been credited to Harshad's account directly, instead of being credited the accounts of UCO Bank.

[52]*Sudhir Shantilal Mehta vs. CBI*, [2009] INSC 1421.

recover their money. The scam still evokes many a passionate memory in the Indian consciousness, be it amongst the investors who lost their money, or the bank employees who faced frequent CBI raids, or the RBI which finally had to realize that its regulatory system had failed. Before his conviction, Harshad had attempted to make a comeback as a market analyst offering stock tips to investors—however, the SEBI banned him for life from the stock markets.

AUTHORS' NOTE

Harshad Mehta continues to be a controversial figure in the history of the Indian capital markets. Many saw him as a forerunner, a man who was trying to work in a system designed against prosperity and progress; others saw him as flamboyant and reckless. The media put Harshad's life under scrutiny and his wealthy, opulent lifestyle was a subject of much debate. Many were quick to blame greed and its associated vices. Others took the view that Harshad just exploited an open loophole in the system in the quest to make more money. The Fort area of Mumbai is not the friendliest place in the world for a small-town boy trying to make it big, and in his desire to succeed, Harshad exploited a loophole that the regulators failed to notice. The regulatory failures that were to blame for Harshad's meteoric rise and fall continue to exist in new forms and many more scams have taken place since then.

KETAN PAREKH:
THE RETURN OF THE BULL

'Bulls make money. Bears make money. Pigs? They get slaughtered.'

—Gordon Gekko, in the movie *Wall Street*

KETAN PAREKH—OR 'KP', as he was popularly known—was a tall and thin Gujarati gentleman with unassuming looks and a humble nature. A chartered accountant by qualification, KP lived close to Marine Drive in Mumbai and worked as a stock broker out of an office in Nariman Bhavan. Though a soft-spoken and shy man, KP's friends circle included famous personalities from the film industry, well-placed politicians, business magnates and other celebrities from Mumbai. KP had a passion for luxury cars and owned a collection of expensive and imported automobiles.

It was the perfect life—he was wealthy, had a happy family and was respected by all those he worked with. On 30 March 2001, the life of this rich, smart and well-connected gentleman changed completely. He was banned from practising his business and doing what he loved most: trading on the stock market. The ban transformed KP's life. Suddenly, the free flow of money became restricted and his so-called friends disappeared.

This is the story of the second Big Bull of India—KP, aka

Ketan Parekh. Having received hands-on training by the Big Bull himself, the late Harshad Mehta, and his brother, Ashwin, Ketan was a legend of a stock broker and was considered a demigod by many in the securities market. He was also referred to as the 'Pied Piper of Dalal Street'—investors followed his every action, since all the stocks he touched seemed to turn to gold.

KP's favourite stocks were called K-10 stocks and they were closely watched by investors. The K-10 stocks were of Aftek, Infosys, DSQ Software, HFCL, Global Tele-Systems Ltd., Pentamedia Graphics Ltd., Ranbaxy Laboratories, Silverline Technologies, Satyam Computers Ltd., SSI Ltd. and Zee Telefilms Ltd. The K-10 stocks were selected by Ketan due to their low liquidity. The buoyant stock markets from January to July 1999 helped these stocks increase in value substantially—HFCL soared by 57 per cent while Global increased by 200 per cent. Mutual funds like Alliance Capital, ICICI Prudential Fund and UTI also invested in K-10 stocks, and saw their net asset value soar. By January 2000, K-10 stocks regularly featured in the top five traded stocks in the exchanges.

The dream run did, however, come to an end. Life changed for KP after the Bank of India filed a complaint against him for defrauding the bank of crores of rupees. It is estimated that KP and his associates had defrauded the Bank of India of ₹137 crore. On 30 March 2001, Lady Luck disappeared from the life of KP and he was arrested by the CBI.[53] He was released on bail on 21 May 2001, but SEBI started investigating, and unearthed even more scams. It was a shocking realization for many that an individual had single-handedly manipulated the

---

[53]'CBI arrests stock broker Ketan Parekh,' *Rediff* (Mumbai, 30 March 2001).

Indian stock market.

ANATOMY OF THE SCAM

KP's modus operandi for the commission of stock-market scams was simple. He operated through a large number of entities, which helped conceal the connection between him and the funds, which originated from corporate houses, banks, financial institutions and foreign institutional investors. The funds received by subsidiary entities from banks as loans and overdrafts were diverted to other subsidiaries for acquiring shares or for meeting other obligations. The purchase and sale of shares was done using the names of a large number of different entities so that the concentration of transactions in a particular scrip could not be readily detected. Various layers of corporate entities were created so that it became difficult to link the source of the funds with the actual users and the end uses to which these fund were put.[54]

The next step was the identification of companies with relatively low-floating stocks. Once this was done, KP used to acquire substantial stocks in these companies either directly or through associates. He controlled the prices and volumes of select scrips by buying and selling them between his own entities, at the price and volumes determined by him, thus indirectly controlling their price and price movements.

When the prices of scrips rose high enough, he pledged the shares with banks as collateral for funds. The Ahmedabad-based Madhavapura Mercantile Cooperative Bank was KP's

---

[54]*Joint Committee on Stock Market Scam and Matters Relating Thereto: Report (Volume 1).* India: Lok Sabha Secretariat, 2002.

main resource in the swindle. The bank used to issue pay orders in favour of Ketan Parekh's entities from time to time, without proper collateral security, which would then discount these pay orders with Bank of India. The stock exchange branch of the bank would present these pay orders for realization to the clearing house in the normal course of their business. On 8 February 2000 and 9 March 2001, the Madhavapura Mercantile Cooperative Bank issued such pay orders totalling ₹137 crore in favour of Ketan Parekh's entities, which were immediately discounted with Bank of India and the proceeds received were utilized by the entities.[55] As per an RBI inspection report, the Madhavapura Mercantile Cooperative Bank's loans to stock markets were around ₹1,000 crore, of which over ₹800 crore was lent to KP and his entities.[56] It was also alleged that the Global Trust Bank issued loans to KP and its exposure to the capital markets was above the prescribed limits.

KP's modus operandi of raising funds by offering shares as collateral security to banks worked well as long as the share prices were rising, but it reversed when the markets started crashing in March 2000. By April 2000, mutual funds substantially reduced their portfolio of K-10 stocks. In December 2000, the NASDAQ crashed again and technology stocks took the toughest beating in the US. Anxiety regarding the future of technology stocks grew, and prices started falling across the globe as mutual funds and brokers began off-loading their stocks. KP began to have liquidity problems and lost a lot of money during that period. The Calcutta Stock Exchange's (CSE) payment crisis was one of

---

[55]*Joint Committee on Stock Market Scam and Matters Relating Thereto: Report (Volume 1)*. India: Lok Sabha Secretariat, 2002.
[56]'The Ketan Parekh Scam,' *Force9* (Blog) (March 2009).

the biggest setbacks for KP. The CSE brokers started pressurizing KP for payments. KP again turned to Madhavapura Mercantile Cooperative Bank to get loans. Finally, KP's resources started drying up and he had no money to clear his debts. Dues to Madhavapura Mercantile Cooperative Bank, Global Trust Bank and several other lending agencies remained unpaid by KP and his entities.

PROBING THE SCAM

The state's response to the Ketan Parekh scam was similar to the reaction to the Harshad Mehta scam: a joint parliamentary committee was set up on 27 April 2001 to investigate the fraud. The committee was led by Prakash Mani Tripathi and consisted of thirty members.

During the investigation, KP was asked whether he had crossed the principles of risk management, to which he said:

'During the year 1999-2000, the companies alleged to be connected or associated with me reported profit of ₹215 crore and paid income tax of about ₹100 crore. My confidence levels in myself escalated and I started building up huge positions in the market, which required me to make large financial commitments. In the hope that my bullishness for India and Indian technology companies will come true, I crossed the principles of risk management and failed miserably. During 2000-01, the technology stocks started losing favour with fears of recession setting in and not only NASDAQ, which is the forefront indicator of investor interest in technology, but all markets across the globe went into a 'bear' phase. In India, given that I was a large investor and had grossly overcommitted myself to the market, many market players started taking advantage of the situation [...] In order to honour my commitments, I raised resources from bank by pledging assets, from corporates by selling my investments and from market intermediaries, etc., which instead of reducing my financial burden, actually deepened the crisis.'[57]

The joint parliamentary committee completed its report on 12 December 2002. The committee found KP to be the key architect of the stock market scam which surfaced in March 2001. The committee also noted that KP was responsible for the payment problem in the CSE and the crash of Madhavpura Mercantile Cooperative Bank. The committee, on the basis of the SEBI report, confirmed that the amount outstanding from Ketan Parekh's entities to certain corporate houses at the end of April 2001 was over ₹1,273 crore. The entities owed Madhavpura Mercantile Cooperative Bank around ₹888 crore and owed Global Trust Bank over ₹266 crore. There were also dues to other entities. The committee urged the government to take all the necessary steps to finalize proceedings against Ketan Parekh's entities, recover the amount from these entities and ensure that suitable action was taken against them without delay.

Several cases were filed against KP and his associated entities for manipulative activities such as synchronized trades, circular trading, creation of artificial volume and benchmarking of the prices of certain scrips by executing non-genuine transactions which were detrimental to the integrity of the securities market. Cases have also been initiated against KP and his entities for violation of the Foreign Exchange Management Act, 1999, the Income Tax Act, 1961, the Indian Penal Code, 1860, etc.

---

[57]*Joint Committee on Stock Market Scam and Matters Relating Thereto: Report (Volume 1)*. India: Lok Sabha Secretariat, 2002.

The SEBI passed an order on 12 December 2003 prohibiting Ketan Parekh, Kartik Parekh (his cousin brother), and a few other associated entities, including Classic Credit Ltd., Panther Fincap and Management Services Ltd., Luminant Investment Ltd., Chitrakut Computers Pvt. Ltd., Saimangal Investrade Ltd., Classic Infin and Panther Investrade Ltd. from trading in the securities market, for a period of fourteen years, i.e., till 2017. The order was made in response to the manipulative practices used by them to create an artificial demand in the price of Lupin Laboratories' scrips.

The above case referred to two show-cause notices that were issued to KP and his entities by the SEBI, following allegations of manipulation of Lupin Laboratories' scrips. SEBI alleged that KP and his entities had caused a significant rise in price and volumes in the Lupin scrips during the period from September to December 1999 on the BSE and NSE.

SEBI established that KP and his entities synchronized trades of the scrip of Lupin Laboratories, by matching the time, rate and quantity of sell-and-buy orders placed through select brokers. This was done to create artificial volumes and an artificial market for Lupin's scrips. KP was also held guilty for rotating the Lupin shares from one KP entity to another, and both were therefore held guilty of circular trading, whereby they induced the general public to invest in the scrips by creating the false impression that large trading in them was taking place. The SEBI held that although the shares of the scrip changed hands during the course of the transaction, it was amply clear that the shares were being rotated from one KP entity to another. The SEBI also stated that it was also clear that each of the entities to which the shares were being transferred was in some manner or the other affiliated to Ketan Parekh himself. Therefore, KP's argument that he himself was not involved in the transactions was dismissed. The SEBI observed:

'Although, the separate acts of individual entities, as they claim, may not have resulted in any aberration of law, I find that the entities which were otherwise also connected with each other have acted in concert. When the corporate personality is being blatantly used as a cloak for fraud or improper conduct, and where the protection of public interest is of paramount importance, it is necessary to lift the corporate veil so as to pass an appropriate order rendering justice. This power of the adjudicating authority has been accepted by the Courts and a specific instance of the same can be found in the decision of the Hon. Supreme Court in *Delhi Development Authority vs. Skipper Construction Pvt. Ltd. and Another.*[58]'

Further, KP and his entities had benchmarked the price of the scrip through synchronized, circular and non-genuine trades. In view of the above, KP and his entities were held guilty under Section 11(4), 11b of the Securities and Exchange Board of India Act, 1992 read with Regulation 11 of Securities and Exchange Board of India (Prohibition of Fraudulent and Unfair Trade Practices Relating to Securities Market) Regulations, 2003 for manipulation of Lupin's scrips and were barred from being associated with the stock exchange in any manner till 12 December 2017.

KP and his entities appealed SEBI's order dated 12 December 2003 before the Securities Appellate Tribunal. The tribunal upheld the order, thereby confirming the market watchdog's ban on KP and his entities in associating with the stock exchange

---

[58]1996 SCC [1] 272.

till 12 December 2017.

THE AFTERTASTE

The allure of the stock market was too strong to resist, especially for the second Big Bull. There are reports that Ketan Parekh still operates in the stock markets in India. On 11 July 2012, during an interview with CNBC TV 18, Sucheta Dalal, Managing Editor, *Moneylife*, and the person who had unearthed the Harshad Mehta and Ketan Parekh scams, criticized the government for its inaction despite being aware that KP still operates in the stock markets.

'This [Ketan Parekh back in the market] bogey is on for a year. The "Intelligence" Bureau bleats every month with the very same names like KS Oils. They tap phones with impunity, submit reports routinely, but nothing happens. Ketan's 14-year ban will soon end, but have we heard about the Finance Ministry or SEBI order to start fresh investigations? Nope [...] Surprisingly, the government and the opposition are studiously silent on the whole issue. And in the meanwhile, Ketan has been permitted to go on a holiday to London. His wife and kid live there anyway and are believed to have taken British citizenship. Meanwhile, Madhavpura Mercantile Coop Bank of Ahmedabad has finally been shut down. This is the bank that Ketan Parekh and cronies looted for over Rs. 1,000 crore [...]'[59]

As on March 2014, Ketan Parekh has been sentenced to two years rigorous imprisonment and has also been imposed with a fine of ₹50,000 by the special CBI court.[60]

---

[59]'Re-discovery of Ketan Parekh?' Sucheta Dalal (11 July 2012).

[60]'Stock broker Parekh sentenced to two years rigorous imprisonment by

The impact of the Ketan Parekh scam still lingers. The Madhavpura Mercantile Cooperative Bank, which had greatly financed KP and his entities, was wound up by the Reserve Bank of India in June 2012.

Many investors have been severely affected by the Ketan Parekh stock scam and some even lost their entire life's savings. A small investor hit by the scam said, 'All my lifetime's savings are gone. I don't know how to feed my family.' [61] KP's only reaction to the scam was 'I made mistakes.'[62]

The Ketan Parekh scam had many further ramifications which affected the lives of hundreds of thousands of people. The Unit Trust of India (UTI) was one of the most popular means through which the middle class could invest in stocks at that time. It had heavily invested in K-10 shares and certain members of the UTI were allegedly involved in buoying such shares. The unravelling of the Ketan Parekh scam eroded the net asset value of the funds under the UTI umbrella and depleted the value of the legendary US-64, a scheme in which a large section of the educated middle-income class in India had invested. This triggered a chain of events that culminated in the split of the erstwhile UTI.

AUTHORS' NOTE

After the Harshad Mehta scam, the government tried to plug the loopholes in the system. But the inadequacy of such attempts was laid bare by Ketan Parekh. The market regulators in India were

---

CBI court', *Economic Times* (New Delhi, 4 March 2014).
[61]'Re-discovery of Ketan Parekh?' Sucheta Dalal (11 July 2012).
[62]'Re-discovery of Ketan Parekh?' Sucheta Dalal (11 July 2012).

caught napping while this fraud was perpetrated and the hard-earned money of small investors was eroded by the manipulation of a select few. However, it should also be pointed out that SEBI took lessons from this and subsequently fortified the regulatory framework to ensure that investors are protected from white-collar crimes.

THE AUTO SHANKAR CASE

*'Freedom of Press is an Article of Faith with us, sanctified by
our Constitution, validated by four decades of freedom and
indispensable to our future as a Nation.'*

—Rajiv Gandhi, Former Prime Minister of India

WHILE MOST HEINOUS crimes compel empathy for the victim,
this case in particular garnered a nationwide constitutional
debate about the freedom of the press versus the right to privacy.

Gauri Shankar, better known by his alias, Auto Shankar,
became infamous overnight. His crimes led to three separate
trials—three death sentences were awarded, as were numerous
life imprisonment sentences. Gauri Shankar hailed from Vellore
district in Tamil Nadu and used to earn his livelihood as a painter.
He came to Chennai in 1974 with his wife Jagdeeshwari, and
began driving an autorickshaw. He also began selling arrack (a
distilled alcoholic drink made from either the fermented sap
of coconut flowers, or sugarcane, grain or fruit), and upon the
success of this venture, moved on to selling other illicit liquors.
Once he had established this business, he handed it over to his
younger brother, Mohan. Shankar had already been introduced
to the world of prostitution since he had served as the auto
driver to several prostitutes. Using these connections, he went
on to establish his own brothel.

He housed most of the prostitutes at the brothel itself, though he would handpick a few whom he considered beautiful, and set them up in different houses as his mistresses. He not only established many such residences for his mistresses, but also married some of them, despite already being married. He married four of the girls brought to him for prostitution— Sumathi, Vijaya, Gauri and Sundari. He would give them jewellery and even went to the extreme of tattooing Gauri's name on his palm.

It was not long before Auto Shankar turned abusive. Vijaya and Gauri left him because of the torture they faced at his hands. Sundari immolated herself because she could no longer stand his abuse. Shankar was known to stub his cigarettes on their skin and practise other inhumane acts. In the meantime, his prostitution business flourished and Shankar established another brothel and set up ten more prostitutes.

The facts of the case that was eventually registered against him are unclear beyond this point and are relatively shrouded in mystery. Though Auto Shankar wrote a memoir, it was never published completely due to the restrictions placed on it.

Mysteriously, in 1988, nine teenage girls went missing from Thiruvanmiyur in Chennai. The police had nearly closed the case, believing that the families, being hard-pressed for money, had sold them to the flesh trade. However, when they interacted with the families, the police were faced with powerful appeals to find the girls, which forced them to reconsider their assumptions. In December, a schoolgirl called Subalakshmi alerted the police about an autorickshaw driver who had attempted to kidnap her in front of a wine shop. Immediately, the police placed undercover personnel in front of the wine shop and caught Auto Shankar within ten days. While undercover, these policemen learned of the ghastly story of Auto Shankar—they were told that an auto rickshaw driver was behind the mysterious disappearances of the nine teenage girls. They also found out that the girls had been abducted, murdered, cremated and their ashes had been disposed off in the Bay of Bengal.

Although this was the popular story that many heard, Auto Shankar was actually tried for the murder of six people over the span of two years—Lalitha, Sudalai, Sampath, Mohan, Govindaraj and Ravi.

In 1987, the series of murders began. Lalitha was one of the ten new prostitutes at Auto Shankar's second brothel and was the first victim. She became romantically involved with Shankar and was accordingly made to live in another building, known as Bommi Ammal at Kalachetra. It was here that she met Sudalai, a friend of Shankar's, who also lived in the same quarters. As it turns out, Sudalai and Lalitha fell in love and wanted to elope. They decided to run away together after stealing ₹7,300 as well as a camera that belonged to Shankar. They did not reveal their plans to anyone. Shankar was furious when he discovered their disappearance, and enlisted all his associates to help him track down the couple.

After a few days of tireless searching, he filed a complaint with a police inspector who later served as a witness for the prosecution. The fervour with which he hunted them down gave rise to rumours that there was more to the relationship between Shankar and Lalitha—it was believed that not only were Lalitha and Shankar romantically involved, but that she was probably one of his numerous wives.

The police successfully found Lalita, and the Pallawaram police brought her to the Tiruvamiyur police station where the complaint had been lodged. Lalita refused to leave with Shankar but he placated the policemen who released her into his custody. He was enraged by her rejection, and unable to bear her betrayal, killed her with his bare hands on 28 October 1987. He strangled her, while his accomplices pinned her down on the floor, holding her hands and legs. It is learnt that after the commission of the crime, he took back all the gold jewellery that he had given her—her anklets, earrings and necklace—and carried her to his liquor godown and buried her.

It was around this time that Sudalai distanced himself from Shankar and started a brothel of his own. Until this point, Shankar had not intended to harm Sudalai. However, when he started to poach Shankar's customers, the latter decided to kill him.

Shankar convinced Sudalai to go with him by car to his house at Periyar Nagar on 28 February 1988. There, he was choked and held down by Shankar's accomplices, Eldin and Shivaji, while Shankar kicked him in the groin until he died. Then he doused the body with petrol, lit a cigarette, and set fire to it with the matchstick. It was later discovered that the remains were swept into a bedsheet and thrown in the back waters beneath the Muttukadu Bridge in Chennai.

His next victim was Ravi. Ravi had heard of what had happened to Sudalai and had tried to use that information against Shankar. There were rumours that he had asked for an auto and had tried to blackmail Shankar about Sudalai's murder. Little did he know that this would prove fatal for him.

The next few killings came soon after, on 29 May 1988. His other three victims—Sampath, Mohan and Govindraj—were known to create a racket with the prostitutes. They would wait outside the Taj Mahal Hotel, where Shankar's prostitutes entertained their customers, and the men would harass them. On this particular occasion, they were apparently drunk, according to eyewitness present at the scene who had also seen Anita, a prostitute, descending from an auto. They had tried to grab her hand, and she had screamed. Mohan, Shankar's younger brother, was in the vicinity and had enquired about what was going on. The three men threatened him. Having heard of the incident, Shankar rushed to the spot with his friends, with causarina sticks in hand. They attacked the three men and dragged them into one of Shankar's illicit arrack shops where they beat them mercilessly until it was no longer clear whether they were dead or alive. Shankar realized that he had taken the game too far and there might be severe repercussions this time. Since they could not leave the three men there, they decided to take them home, dump them in the storeroom and lock the doors. However, there were too many witnesses this time. They had come to their house soaked in blood and no number of threats could make his neighbours forget the sight.

A few hours later, at 10.00 p.m., Shankar, Mohan and two others opened the storeroom door. They discovered that two of the men had died, and the other was found murmuring from shock and pain. Shankar quickly strangled him as well, as he believed that it would be unsafe to leave him alive. Their bodies were taken to a construction site and buried.

On 31 May 1988, the brother and relative of two of Shankar's victims, Mohan and Govindraj—who later became Prosecution Witness No. 15—went to the police station to file a complaint. When he explained the circumstances under which his family had gone missing, the police said that they had not heard of any such happening and refused to file a formal complaint. The complainants then went to the Abhiramapuram police station and filed a 'missing man' report there.

Shankar was arrested and soon after, provided a confessional statement. He explained where the bodies were buried and they were exhumed—one by one the pieces of the puzzle fell into place. Shankar's younger brother Mohan was also arrested and his confession was also recorded by the Tehsildar. They also exhumed the bodies of Lalitha and Ravi—the post-mortem report of these corpses revealed that they were killed by strangulation.

Auto Shankar was charged and tried for as many as six murders. The prosecution arranged for 134 witnesses to testify against him and his accomplices. Amongst the witnesses were nine magistrates and five police inspectors. The charge sheet ran to 1,100 pages and covered six major sections of the IPC?

While the trial was on in August 1990, Shankar and his associates escaped detention with the help of jail wardens, but were found soon after and arrested. Auto Shankar was convicted and sentenced to death by the Chengalpattu Sessions Court along with his two associates, Eldin and Shivaji, on 31 May 1991. This conviction and punishment was confirmed by the Madras High Court on 17 July 1992. His appeal to the Supreme Court was dismissed on 5 April 1994, and his mercy petition to the President of India was rejected.

As explained earlier, the death penalty is used as a punishment in the rarest of rare cases. The court discussed it in great detail, while deliberating whether a life imprisonment term would suffice. Finally, however, the courts were unanimous in their conviction and awarded death sentences to Shankar and his two accomplices who had heartlessly killed six people.

The Supreme Court stated the following about his crime:

'[…] The crime indulged in was gruesome, cold-blooded, heinous, atrocious and cruel and he has proved to be an ardent criminal and thus a menace to society. It is an exceptional case where the crime committed by him is so gruesome, diabolical and revolting that it shocks the collective conscience of the community. There cannot be any doubt that his case is one of the rarest of rare cases fully warranting the imposition of death sentence [...][63]

In 2002, Shankar's five other accomplices were sentenced to six months of rigorous imprisonment after having been found guilty by a magistrate. The accomplices were Shankar's brother, Mohan; Selva alias Selvaraj; and the jail wardens Kannan, Balan and Rahim Khan. They were found guilty of criminal conspiracy and resistance or obstruction by a person to his lawful apprehension.

Subsequently, Shankar's younger brother, Auto Mohan, was also found guilty of the six murders and was awarded three life sentences to be served consecutively. Mohan and Selvaraj, who had earlier escaped from the Chennai Central Prison in August 1990, were re-arrested in Pune on 25 June 1992, and in Mumbai on August 20, 1993 respectively.

Auto Shankar, in his last month in jail, revealed some information that shocked the nation. He stated that his actual business had been to procure girls for politicians who raped them and the bodies were disposed of by Shankar.

When Shankar was in prison, he wrote his autobiography describing the entire story of his life of crime. He handed the manuscript over to his wife to be published in the Tamil magazine, *Nakkheeran*. The magazine, in a run-up to the story, publicized the next issue by saying that they were going to

---

[63]*Shankar vs. State of Tamil Nadu*, 1994 SCC (4) 478 57.

come out with the sensational story of Auto Shankar and reveal tremendous secrets.

This information allegedly terrified the local politicians. They feared that their illegal activities would be revealed to the world. They put pressure on Shankar in prison to retract his permission to publish the story. Although several documents exist as proof that he had initially submitted his story for publication, he was forced to withdraw his consent. Although political pressure was evident, it was no longer possible to publish the story without violating his right to privacy. The magazine promptly filed a case against this violation of the freedom of press.

It was argued that the freedom of the press is a fundamental right in a free and democratic society. On the other hand, the court was forced to consider the fact that the author of the autobiography, Shankar, had withdrawn his consent to the publishing of the content. Therefore, as a compromise, the court decided that only the content found in public records can be published and anything further would be in violation of the right of privacy.

Despite the hue and cry over the contents of the autobiography, no investigations were conducted on the involvement of any politician. The media was also wounded in the process of this case—Shankar claimed, as did some police personnel, that the media influenced people adversely by making crime look attractive. Shankar went on to say that the murders he had committed were instigated by the media. He faulted movies for 'making a devil of him'.

Amnesty International, during his trial and prior to his hanging, displayed on its website statistics that proved that often the persons held liable for crimes are scapegoats and are often poor and illiterate. It implored the public to submit their objection to this death sentence, especially via hanging.

Is it possible that we may not have known the whole truth about this case? Have those in power concocted their own version for the events that took place in the years 1987-88, so that they would be safe while someone else took the fall? This mystery will remain unsolved. Shankar was hanged to death on 27 April 1995 at the Salem Central Prison.

AUTHORS' NOTE

This case is one in a series of high-profile cases where the Indian criminal justice system failed to protect the common man from the powers of the high and mighty. Equality before the law is increasingly being perceived as theoretical. However, as we will see later in this book, seminal changes in the attitude of the middle class and the eruption of a modern civilian-led protest many years later started a new trend.

THE BEST BAKERY CASE

'From fanaticism to barbarism is only one step.'

—Denis Diderot

RARELY HAS AN event shocked the conscience of the nation nor stirred the emotion and faith of the people as the incidents and trials related to the Best Bakery catastrophe in the Gujarat of 2002.

The turn of the millennium saw one of the greatest modern human tragedies in India—when more than fifty Hindu pilgrims were burnt alive in a train in Godhra. Before the people of India could recover from the tragedy, riots broke out across Gujarat and right-wing Hindu nationalists sought fanatic retribution in the name of religion. The sheer scale of human atrocity was bloodcurdling, not merely to the victims of the terror, but to the entire nation.

The state of Gujarat boasts of several landmarks and achievements: it has the longest coastline in India and it is the birthplace of Mahatma Gandhi, the father of the nation and the harbinger of peace. It has one of the most industrious business communities in the world, it is the last home of the Asiatic lion, and it houses the historic Somnath temple. However, for a better part of the last decade, Gujarat attracted the world's attention for reasons that are vastly different from the treasures of this vibrant state. Gujarat was the site of one of the worst communal riots seen in India post Partition. The media beamed images of the carnage to television screens across the world. Riotous mobs ran through the streets with swords, they destroyed property and killed hundreds of people—the riots in the land of Gandhi became famous for their violence. The state's right-wing Chief Minister, Narenda Modi, became the focus of attention. Critics claimed that the riots were state-sponsored and state-supported. Hundreds had died and trials were essential. A bleeding country demanded justice.

The trials were, however, mired in controversy. One of the most famous trials of the Gujarat riots was the one of those responsible for the murders at Best Bakery in Vadodara. The trial has since come to be known as the Best Bakery case. Many considered this case to be the test case for the Indian judicial system to show the world it was capable of handling post-conflict scenarios.

THE INCIDENT: AS WE HEARD IT

The death of the fifty-nine Hindus in the Godhra train was largely blamed on Muslim miscreants, and in a vitriolic reaction, the sizeable Muslim minority in the state was cornered by rioting Hindus.

From 8.30 p.m. on 1 March 2002, to 11 a.m. on the next day, a motely crowd went on a rampage, attacking, looting and eventually burning down a residential building and a bakery of a Muslim family in Vadodara. Fourteen people were killed at Best Bakery—twelve Muslims and two others. Though the number appears small compared to the total number of dead at the end of the Gujarat riots, this case would come to symbolize everything that went wrong with the post-riot investigation, the fallibility of the judicial system, and most of all, it would keep in the public imagination the horrors of the riots for years to come.

THE LAW TAKES ITS, ALBEIT STRANGE, COURSE

Zaheera Sheikh, the daughter of the owner of the bakery, filed an FIR regarding the incident on 2 March 2002, the next day. A survivor of the carnage, she decided to seek justice from the state. Just a day earlier, she had seen her life burn down in front of her eyes. She was an eyewitness to the case, so her testimony would be the key evidence to decide the case. A nineteen-year-old Zaheera appeared before the National Human Rights Commission (NHRC) demanding justice on 21 March 2002.[64] The other key witness in the case was a man called Qutubuddin Ansari. Unlike Zaheera, his name does not readily ring a bell in most people's minds. But this tailor's face is etched in the memory of most Indians. On 2 March 2002, most of India woke up to see a photo of a man begging the police to save him from the mob. Qutubuddin Ansari, with his hands pleading and the fear of God in his eyes was, perhaps, for most of India and the world, the embodiment of the horrors of the Gujarat riots.[65]

THE TRIAL OR TRIALS

A well-accepted principle of criminal law is that the court in whose area the crime is committed, or the court that first

---

[64]'Chronology of events in Best Bakery Case,' *Rediff* (India, 24 February 2006).

[65]'Best Bakery: Why is it so important,' *Rediff* (India, 24 February 2006).

learns of the crime, is the court that has the right to try the said crime. Courts are usually present in each district of a state. The criminal cases of a district are to be tried by the sessions court of that district. The sessions court reports to the High Court of that state. In some cases, however, special courts may be created on a fast-track basis to solve matters of urgent public importance. The special courts are usually presided by a High Court judge, handle only specific matters and have a limited existence just for the duration of the trial. They are created to ensure speedy conviction or acquittal in cases where the public or the government have a major stake. All the cases connected to the Gujarat riots were tried by a special fast-track court set up specifically for that purpose. This was to ensure that the cases would be processed speedily and society would be able to quickly move on from the horrors of the trial. However, in the Best Bakery case, it would soon become evident that this system was not as foolproof as it was once thought to be.

In our system of justice, seldom is an accused punished without there being overwhelming evidence against him. It is the burden of the prosecution to establish 'beyond all reasonable doubt' that the accused is guilty. This has been implanted into our judicial system in order to safeguard the liberty of the people—it has to be ensured that justice is not only done, but is *seen* to be done. It is a golden thread that runs through our legal system. The burden to prove a crime is always on the side of the accuser, the prosecution. Each accusation needs to be substantiated, to ensure that only the right person is convicted of the crime and no innocent person is punished. It is accepted that the court may release a hundred people whose guilt is not conclusively proved, rather than punish someone about whose guilt the court is not convinced 'beyond all reasonable doubt'.

This principle was put to the test in the Best Bakery case. The nation was more or less certain about the verdict that the court should deliver. However, the events that occurred are as follows:

Twenty-one persons were accused in the Best Bakery case and on 27 June 2003, the special court acquitted all of them for lack of evidence. Thirty-seven of the seventy-three witnesses turned hostile, i.e., they were presented by the prosecution but ended up testifying to the contrary. It was during this proceeding that Zaheera herself turned hostile. She said that she had been hiding while the massacre took place and had not seen what had happened.

The nation was shocked. People were expecting justice from the fast-track court in Gujarat. What they got instead was an acquittal. The state government gave the Gujarat police a rap on the knuckles for conducting a shoddy investigation and the verdict was appealed before the Gujarat High Court.

Less than a month later, Zaheera appeared after taking an oath before the NHRC, stating that she had been facing death threats and had been coerced to change her testimony. The NHRC, being the body responsible for the protection of human rights in the country, can intervene in cases and take them up to ensure that human rights are being respected. It therefore took cognizance of the matter and filed a petition before the Supreme Court in Delhi asking that the case be moved out of Gujarat for trial.

Upon hearing both, the petition by the NHRC and the appeal by the Gujarat government, the Supreme Court, relying on a sworn statement by Zaheera that her life was in danger, ordered that the case be tried outside Gujarat, and shifted the venue of the trial to the neighbouring state of Maharashtra.

While the power to shift a trial rests solely with the Supreme Court, it is one that is used very rarely and sparingly. Such an order makes the state from which the trial has been moved look incompetent in performing an essential function of civil society and reflects poorly on the law and order prevalent in that state. However, in this case, the honourable judges of the Supreme Court thought it best that the case be moved to Mumbai. Many in Gujarat also took this move as a personal insult to the state, and felt that as a community they were being targetted by media propaganda.

ALL EYES ON MUMBAI

Things changed once the case was moved to Mumbai and more witnesses testified. However, Zaheera turned hostile once again. She again said that she had not seen anything and alleged that she was being coerced by Tessta Setalvad, a prominent social activist who was spearheading the campaign to bring justice to victims of the riots. This went down well with the people of Gujarat, who felt that NGOs and social activists were simply out to malign the state and its government. Narendra Modi tapped into this anxiety extensively in his state election campaign, to great success.

Around the same time, investigative magazine *Tehelka* published an exposé, where Zaheera was seen receiving a bribe of ₹18 lakh by Madhu Srivastava, a BJP MLA from Gujarat. In response, the Muslim community in India discredited her and the Majlis-e-Shura declared her an 'outsider', stating that she had brought shame to India's Muslim community.

In 2006, the court in Mumbai convicted nine of the twenty-one accused of murder and sentenced them to life imprisonment.

At the same time, it acquitted eight others and issued arrest warrants for four other missing persons. The nine filed an appeal with the high court in Mumbai and, in 2012, the court acquitted five of them for want of evidence. Even after an intervention by the Supreme Court and efforts made to smoothen the judicial process, there was only enough evidence to convict four people. Once again, this was played up by the media and was used as an example to show the incompetence of the investigation and the Gujarat police.

Under evidence law, a person who testifies before a court must first swear an oath, usually on a religious text, declaring that the statements they make in court are true. Statements made under oath are presumed true, unless proven otherwise. If a person intentionally makes a false statement when under oath, they can be punished for the crime of perjury. Zaheera was convicted of perjury and sentenced to a year's imprisonment and fined ₹50,000. Perjury, or lying under oath, is one of the more serious offences that a person can commit as it will directly lead to a miscarriage of justice. The fact that Zaheera was also sentenced to jail, in a case where she was also the victim, sheds light on the fact that the judicial system does not care about who committed the crime, but enforces the law as it stands.

AUTHORS' NOTE

The Best Bakery case exposed many of the flaws in India's judicial system, from the series of acquittals to the fact that witnesses could keep changing their statements. It was a judicial nightmare, to say the least. Public confidence in the courts was shaken, and the media only made it worse by pointing out to a nation recovering from riots the fallibility of its justice system.

It also showed how vulnerable the Indian judicial system is to outside influence. From accusations of bribing and intimidation of witnesses, which led to changed statements during the trial, the case exposed the system to public scrutiny.

What seems to be the most interesting element in this case, however, is the fact that Zaheera, a victim, was swayed by pressure and bribery to change her statements. If anything, this case should teach us that it is high time India focuses on victims' rights and introduces a witness protection program. Victims and witnesses are exposed to intimidation and pressure, which affects the integrity and efficacy of the judicial process.

The trial did not close the chapter on the Gujarat riots—there are still many cases pending and many more crimes to be resolved. It did, however, set the process in motion and allowed for the judicial system to try and rein in what had gone so horribly wrong in the country.

It also showed that the Indian judiciary was independent and capable of delivering justice. It tends to be a tad delayed, is shaky on many occasions, but is nevertheless capable of handling high-profile, politically sensitive criminal trials where communal tensions abound.

The Vishakha Case

'The more you face the truth, the angrier you will probably become. You have a right to be angry about being sexually abused. You have a right to be angry with the perpetrator, regardless of who it was, how long ago the sexual abuse occurred, or how much he/she has changed.'

—Beverly Engel, *The Right to Innocence*

INDIAN SOCIETY HAS come a long way since independence more than sixty years ago. Women who were earlier confined to domestic spaces are now at the forefront of India's young and modern workforce, competing for the same jobs and earning the same wages as their male counterparts.

However, it cannot be said that the attitude towards women has changed everywhere in India. Women are victims of various forms of sexual violence, starting from the roadside 'eve teasing' to brutal rapes and murders. Various reports of crimes against women feature regularly in the news. The safety of women is a growing concern across the country. After the horrific gang rape and murder of a young woman in December 2012 in New Delhi, there has been extreme public outrage across the nation.

As more and more women enter the workplace, the need for gender equality and security measures within organizations has never been more significant. Sexual harassment at work is commonplace, and more often than not is swept under the carpet. The victim is usually left with the choice of either dealing with the harassment herself, or leaving the job.

The judgment of the Supreme Court in *Vishaka vs. State of Rajasthan* ('Vishakha Judgment')[66] on 13 August 1997 defines sexual harassment at workplaces and lays down the guidelines to be followed to prevent it. The Sexual Harassment of Women at Workplace (Prevention, Prohibition and Redressal) Act 2013 was brought into effect on 22 April 2013, following ratification of the International Convention of the Elimination of All Forms of Discrimination against Women by India in 1993 and the Vishakha judgment.

BHANWARI DEVI

Bhanwari Devi is a woman from Bhateri, fifty-five kilometres from Jaipur, Rajasthan. In 1985, she joined the Women's Development Project (WDP) run by the government of Rajasthan as a 'saathin', a ground-level worker. As part of her job, she had to educate and inform people about issues like education, water, health, minimum wages, etc.

In 1992, she clashed with some higher-caste 'Gurjar' families in her village when she tried to stop a child from being married off. A nine-month old child was to be married off. Bhanwari's attempts to persuade the family fell upon deaf ears, so she approached the police. The officers stalled the marriage for the time being, but could not save Bhanwari Devi from the aftermath of her deeds.

She was boycotted socially by the villagers and her own family members. Then on 22 September 1992, it was reported

---

[66]*Vishaka & Ors vs. State of Rajasthan & Ors*, JT 1997(7) SC 384.

that six villagers attacked Bhanwari's husband, struck him unconscious and gang raped her.

THE VISHAKHA JUDGMENT

Following the rape, several women's organizations joined hands and filed a public interest litigation (PIL) under the collective platform of 'Vishakha'. The State of Rajasthan and the Union of India were made parties in the case. The petitioners urged the court to take steps to curb sexual harassment at the workplace since the State has failed its obligation to protect women.

There was no law against sexual harassment in India, no guidelines to prevent it and no mechanism to redress grievances faced by many women across the country. The hung parliament at the centre proved to be unhelpful in framing any legislation to protect women at the workplace. Therefore, the Supreme Court was approached.

India is a common law country—the judgments of the superior courts have the force of law. Article 141 of the Constitution entrenches this principle and states that the law declared by the Supreme Court shall be applicable in India. Therefore, the directions given by the Supreme Court with regard to certain issues gain the force of law. The Supreme Court may exercise this power as it deems fit, upon its sole discretion. Some countries call this system judicial law-making, others call it judicial overreach; in India, the Supreme Court has utilized this power sparingly but effectively from time to time.

Rather than fighting as adversaries, the parties in this case got together in order to find a solution to the problem of sexual harassment in the workplace.

The Supreme Court began by referring to the fundamental

rights guaranteed in the Constitution of India. It stated that the right to practise any trade or profession along with the right to life included the right to a safe work environment, and if this was not provided, the constitutional rights of women across the country were being violated.

The Supreme Court said that since the Constitution guaranteed protection against sexual harassment, there is a need for a law to deal with this subject matter. Because of the lack of a specific law to address this, the court began to refer to international conventions to which India was a party. Since these conventions, namely the Convention for the Elimination of Discrimination Against Women, were in harmony with our Constitution, the Supreme Court sought to broaden the fundamental rights in this regard.

Further, the Supreme Court drafted certain guidelines which it promulgated with the consent of the central government. The guidelines were announced via its judgment in order to ensure the prevention of sexual harassment in the workplace and the creation of a grievance redress mechanism for the same.

GUIDELINES

The guidelines of the Supreme Court established that it was the duty of the employer to prevent sexual harassment in the workplace. It also stated that every workplace shall have a grievance redress mechanism by way of a committee headed by a woman and half its members also being women. The committee may involve counsellors and should engage with local NGOs. The complaints to the committee are to be kept strictly confidential. Further, the committee should provide a report to the government regarding the action it has taken over the year.

The guidelines also call for discussions between employers and employees about sexual harassment issues.

The Supreme Court issued these guidelines under Article 142 of the Constitution. The article empowers the Supreme Court to pass any order it sees fit to meet the ends of justice. After the judgment in this case was announced, the guidelines became law and everyone was required to comply.

IMPACT

The impact of this case can be analysed from several viewpoints. The first and foremost being the Supreme Court's role in interpreting our Constitution in a liberal manner, which includes allowing a wide variety of rights not specifically mentioned in the original text, to take shape. This enables a broad reading of the various provisions of the Constitution in light of an evolving Indian society. The case highlights how the Supreme Court, through its interpretations, has allowed for the basic intentions of the framers to take precedence over the cold letter of the law, truly allowing our Constitution to be rightfully called a living Constitution, a being that adapts to the changing facets of the reality around it.

The case also highlights how blurred the line between parliament and the courts can be. Our Constitution provides for a doctrine known as the separation of powers—the parliament makes the law, the executive enforces it and the judiciary interprets the law as and when there is a dispute. These lines become blurred when the Supreme Court chooses to enter what is clearly the domain of the legislature. In this case, since there was clearly a void in the legal framework, and since India was expected to follow the Convention of the Elimination of All

Forms of Discrimination Against Women, the Supreme Court stepped in to frame the regulations.

It would be wrong to assume that the Supreme Court intended the guidelines to be made permanent laws against sexual harassment; it was rather a temporary stop-gap measure. This probably justifies the fact that the guidelines provide for no penalty for violators, thereby enabling the provisions of existing laws, especially the IPC, to operate until the parliament frames a new law to address the issue.

It took the parliament about sixteen years to frame the much-needed law and it enacted the Sexual Harassment of Women at Workplace (Prevention, Prohibition and Redressal) Act in 2013. The Supreme Court also framed its own internal guidelines to prevent sexual harassment within the court complex and instructed all the High Courts to follow suit. It is ironic that it took the Supreme Court sixteen years to set up its own mechanism to prevent sexual harassment, though it had passed the Vishaka judgment in 1997.

AUTHORS' NOTE

In conclusion, the case of *Vishaka vs. State of Rajasthan* set a landmark precedent in the field of women's rights in India. The judgment was welcomed by many international agencies, and many courts in the Commonwealth countries have incorporated the guidelines into their own respective case laws. The case has come to be one of the most respected precedents ever made by an Indian court. This case, along with the Chandrima Das case, is proof that the Indian judiciary can be vigilant in protecting the most vulnerable, and this is one of the most significant judgments in India's long road to modernity.

THE CHANDRIMA DAS CASE

'She couldn't get any farther away inside from her skin. She couldn't get away.'

—Cynthia Voigt, *When She Hollers*

THE GANG RAPE of the young physiotherapy student in December 2012 in New Delhi set off a flurry of legislative changes in India. Following public outcry, 2013 turned into a significant year for legislations relating to sexual crimes in India. The Sexual Harassment of Women at Workplace (Prevention, Prohibition and Redressal) Act 2013 was enacted and the Criminal Law (Amendment) Ordinance 2013 was promulgated by the president. The ordinance provides for amendment of the IPC, Code of Criminal Procedure and Indian Evidence Act, on laws relating to sexual offences.

However, before the legislature took notice of the need for stronger laws for sexual offences, the courts in India had consistently taken strong stands in such cases over the last two decades. Along with the Vishaka judgment, the Chandrima Das case is another instance where the courts have attempted to address sexual offences and introduce institutional reform.

THE FACTS

Hanufa Khatun was from Bangladesh. She arrived at Kolkata on 24 February 1998 and stayed at a hotel in the city for two days. She then decided to visit Ajmer Sharif, the shrine of the Sufi saint Moinuddin Chishti located in Ajmer, Rajasthan. Hanufa arrived at Howrah Railway Station at 2.00 p.m. on 26 February 1998, with the intention of boarding the Jodhpur Express. Since she had a waitlisted ticket, she approached the ticket examiner to ask if there was a berth available. The examiner requested her to wait in the ladies' waiting room. At about 5.00 p.m., two men approached her while she was waiting and, claiming to be ticket touts, said they would help her get a reservation.

At 8.00 p.m., the men returned with a reservation under her name. One of them, Siya Ram Singh, offered to accompany her to dinner at a nearby restaurant. After eating the food there she vomited; this was at around 9.00 p.m. After a while, Ashoke Singh, the other tout, met her at the waiting room along with another person called Rafi Ahmed, a parcel supervisor. He offered to take her to Yatri Nivas, the railway rest house. After the lady attendant at the waiting room certified the credentials of both these men, she went with them to Yatri Nivas.

She was taken to Room 102, which had been booked under the name of Ashoke Singh. Sitaram Singh, an employee of the electric department of the station, joined them on the way. Two other men joined them in the room—Lalan Singh, a parcel clerk of the station, and Awdesh Singh, a parcel clearing agent. Ashoke Singh forced Hanufa into the room and Awdesh Singh locked the door from outside and stood guard. The men began drinking and forced her to drink as well. Hanufa was violently raped in that room.

When she recovered, Hanufa managed to escape and went back to the platform where she found Siya Ram Singh talking to Ashoke Singh. The former, after hearing the story, abused and slapped Ashoke Singh. It was midnight and the Jodhpur train had already departed. Siya Ram Singh told her that he would take her to his house where she would be safe; he lied to her and told her that his wife would be there. He said that he would put her on a train the next morning. When Hanufa went to his house, Siya Ram Singh gagged her mouth and raped her. The landlord of the building informed the police after Hanufa raised a hue and cry and woke the neighbours.

The events of that night alone are enough to horrify the average conscience; the fact that government employees in a government building perpetrated it makes it all the more shocking.

Chandrima Das was an advocate practising in Kolkata. Upon hearing of the incident, she filed a writ petition[67] against the central government and the railway board for compensation, as she claimed that Hanufa's fundamental rights were breached.

HIGH COURT

The petition under was filed Article 226 of the Constitution on behalf of Hanufa in the Calcutta High Court, claiming that since the rape was perpetrated by railway employees in a railway rest house, the central government and the railways were liable to pay compensation to the victim. The High Court agreed and awarded compensation of ₹10 lakh. The government appealed to the Supreme Court against the verdict.

---

[67] *The Chairman, Railway Board & Ors vs. Mrs. Chandrima Das & Ors.*, AIR 2000 SC 988.

THE SUPREME COURT

The government claimed that since Hanufa was only an individual affected by the action, she is not eligible to approach the court under Article 226. Article 226, the government said, was only for 'public wrongs', and since this was a 'private wrong', her claim for compensation should be made in front of district courts. The court rejected this argument and said that Article 32 and Article 226 covers every action by the State, including actions against one individual alone. The court can review such actions or inaction in the exercise of its powers. The court stated that the case before them was no ordinary case, but involved the violation of a very important fundamental right—the right to life guaranteed in the Constitution. It went on to state:

> 'Where public functionaries are involved and the matter relates to the violation of fundamental rights or the enforcement of public duties, the remedy would still be available under the public law notwithstanding that a suit could be filed for damages under private law. In the instant case, it is not a mere matter of violation of an ordinary right of a person but the violation of fundamental rights which is involved. Smt. Hanufa Khatun was a victim of rape.[68]'

The court further cited an earlier ruling and stated that:

> 'Rape is a crime not only against the person of a woman; it is a crime against the entire society. It destroys the entire psychology of a woman and pushes her into deep

---

[68] *The Chairman, Railway Board & Ors vs. Mrs Chandrima Das & Ors.*, AIR 2000 SC 988.

emotional crisis. Rape is therefore the most hated crime. It is a crime against basic human rights and is violative of the victim's most cherished right, namely, the right to life which includes the right to live with human dignity contained in Article 21.'

The court held that such a matter was clearly within the domain of public law and what had been committed was public wrong that deserved a remedy, dismissing the contention of the government that Article 226 was not the appropriate remedy.

The second point raised by the government in its appeal to the Supreme Court was that Chandrima Das had no *locus standi*—that no third party had the right to file a petition on her behalf. The court rejected the argument and referred to her original petition as being one that not only covered that particular incident, but also sought to clean up the den of criminals at the Howrah Railway Station. The court held that this petition was clearly PIL and that that rule could be done away with in this present case.

The government raised another objection and claimed that since Hanufa was a foreign national, she was not entitled to file a writ petition against the government of India. It claimed that the government had no duty towards foreign nationals. The court resoundingly rejected this argument. Relying on the Universal Declaration of Human Rights, which it described as a 'model moral code of conduct for nations', the court stated that a person could not be denied their rights on the basis of their nationality or political status. It further went on to analyse the rights of an individual under the Constitution. While it said some rights were only limited to citizens, some rights were available to all persons regardless of their citizenship status. The right to life being one such right, and therefore, the government was obligated to ensure that Hanufa's right to life was respected, regardless of the fact that she was from Bangladesh and not India. Since this event had occurred in India, it was the duty of the government to ensure her safety and it had failed to deliver on that duty.

In a final desperate argument before the court, the government contended that it could not be held liable for the acts of its employees. It relied on the doctrine of vicarious liability, a doctrine under the law of torts, that one person can only be held liable for the actions of another if they have the power to control that person's actions. The court said that the government was liable for the actions of its employees. It said that in a welfare state such as India, the role of the government was extensive and extends to many spheres. The government could not claim that the running of railways, being a commercial activity, was not a state function, and therefore shrug off responsibility. In a welfare state, the government had many obligations to perform and running the railways was one such obligation. Therefore, when railway employees committed such horrible acts on railway property, while on duty, the government could be held liable for their actions. The perpetrators of the crime used their official position to get the room booked and their official position was also used to trick Hanufa into going to the room with them. Therefore, the State was liable and damages had to be paid.

The Supreme Court thus upheld the verdict of the High Court and instructed the government to pay Hanufa the compensation she deserved, being the sum of ₹10 lakh. At the end, Hanufa was paid her compensation via the High Commissioner for Bangladesh in India. The railways were held liable and the State now realized it could be sued for such lapses.

CONCEPT OF LOCUS STANDI

Locus standi is a concept in law that states that only a party who has an interest in the matter may file a case. For example, if there is a dispute between A and B, then C cannot sue anyone regarding the fight as C was not a party to the case. This rule essentially exists to prevent frivolous litigation. However, the rule has undergone significant change in India, as the Supreme Court has relaxed it in order to allow a public-spirited individual to champion public causes in courts. This is now commonly known as PIL. These litigations allow any public-minded person to approach the courts under Article 32 and Article 226 to seek remedy on behalf of the general public, since in many instances the aggrieved persons may not have the means to undertake such an endeavour themselves.

IMPACT

Money can never really compensate a wrong such as rape that affects the consciousness of an individual and scars her for the rest of her life—but it is a way to make reparations for the same. The compensation was awarded because sometimes money helps smoothen the process by which a victim may return to her life. However, this is not why the case has such significance.

The fear of being sued leads institutions and its employees to act more responsibly. It acts as a deterrence the same way the threat of punishment stops an individual from committing crimes. The government is an artificial entity, and therefore cannot be locked up in jail for its crimes. Individuals can be put behind bars for their individual crimes but one cannot punish an entire system under the criminal law. So, a severe financial penalty may act as a deterrent for an organization, even if it is the government, if it fails to do its duty.

This case is significant as it states that the government can be sued and be held liable if it fails to protect the life on an individual. It forces the State to work towards ensuring the safety of each person. The threat of financial damages is the only whip that a people have to ensure a system does not stray from the purpose for which it was founded.

Another significant feature of this case is that it recognized the fact that a person, regardless of his or her national origin, is entitled to protection in India. India, being a civilized country, cannot shirk its responsibilities merely because the affected person is not an Indian citizen. What happened to Hanufa at that station was a gross injustice and she deserved remedy for what went wrong. The Indian government has a duty to ensure that all persons in India are treated with dignity and they are given a chance to lead a dignified life. Rape, being an offence against the dignity of a person, should be prevented by the State.

The case also imposes liability on the government for the actions of its employees. In an age where police brutality and violence on the part of enforcement officials is becoming common, it is important to hold the system as a whole liable for the failures of its functionaries. This ensures that the system takes steps to remedy its flaws and allows for a modicum of compensation to be paid to the victims of such lapses by the State.

AUTHORS' NOTE

Given the fact that the rate of violence against women has clearly risen in India since 1998, doubt prevails if the Chandrima Das ruling actually served as a deterrent, or if it was like any other judicial decision of the past, only a speck of dust in a long list of crimes against women. However, it would be pertinent to mention that along with the Vishakha judgment, this was a milestone in the battle for safety of women in India. The courts can only provide justice on a case-to-case basis and try to set precedents that may act as a deterrent to future criminals. To that extent this was a laudable decision.

MANU SHARMA:
THE JESSICA LAL MURDER

'Distrust all in whom the impulse to punish is powerful.'

—Freidrich Neitzche

IF THERE WAS a story that defined the year 2006 for most Indians, it was the hue and cry over the murder of Jessica Lal and the trial that ensued. The Jessica Lal murder case was the coming of age moment for India's news media and will continue to live on in the national memory as the first time public opinion was shaped, channelled and used by the media to expedite the judicial process. It was this case that made the phrase 'trial by media' part of the common vocabulary of most Indians.

WHO WAS JESSICA LAL?

Jessica Lal was a model based in Delhi. She also worked as a celebrity barmaid at high-profile parties. On 29 April 1999, Jessica was working at a party hosted at an upmarket restaurant called Tamarind Court in Delhi's posh Qutub Colonnade complex. The party was hosted by a popular socialite, Bina Ramani, who was a UK citizen. It was ostensibly a farewell party for her husband, but later it was found that the party was open to anyone who was willing to pay for it. Bina Ramani as well as her husband were later charged with operating an illegal bar and their passports were impounded by the Delhi Court.

At around 2.00 a.m., Siddharth Vashisht, who was commonly known by his alias, Manu Sharma, asked Jessica for a drink. When she informed him that the alcohol had run out, in full public view, he took his .22 calibre pistol, fired one shot into the air and another straight into her head. She was rushed to Apollo Hospital where she was declared dead. Manu Sharma and his friends fled the scene in their Tata Safari and for the next few weeks, tried to keep a low-profile, after the police investigation had commenced.

On 6 May 1999, Manu Sharma surrendered before a Chandigarh Court; he could not be placed into custody immediately as he had already secured anticipatory bail. Another co-accused in the case, Vikas Yadav, was also arrested. Vikas was the son of powerful UP politician, D.P. Yadav. The case was committed to trial by the Delhi sessions court.

THE INITIAL TRIAL

In India, criminal trials happen in an adversarial manner and the prosecution has to prove its case beyond all reasonable doubt. In this trial, the prosecution relied on the testimonies of witnesses present at the party in order to establish proof of events. Shayan Munshi, who had been an up-and-coming Bollywood actor back in 1999, and is now quite a popular face, deposed before the court and turned hostile by failing to identify Manu Sharma.

According to *Black's Law Dictionary* (Second Edition), a 'hostile witness' is defined as, 'a party that the court feels is hostile against the party they are supposed to testify for. They can be cross-examined if they are called.'[69] In this case, Shayan Munshi was to be a key witness for the prosecution. However, he ended up aiding the case of the accused through his testimony. Shiv Das and Karan Rajput, who were the other key eyewitnesses in the case, also turned hostile. It was only Bina Ramani, who had organized the party, and her daughter, Malini Ramani, who identified Manu Sharma. As a result, the trial proceeded at a slow pace and the court acquitted the accused in 2006 due to lack of evidence. In India, even if a judge's instinct leads him to believe that an accused is guilty, unless he is presented with substantial evidence to support the theory, the judge must acquit the accused. In this case, it was clear that the prosecution had been unable to discharge its burden of proof beyond all reasonable doubt since the hostile witnesses had refused to testify to having seen the crime.

REACTIONS

The Indian middle class' anger over the judicial process reached a tipping point when the verdict of the trial court in the Jessica Lal case was announced. The judicial process in India is plagued by many issues, starting from the corruption of police officers to the slow and long-drawn-out trials before India's snail-paced judiciary. Victims and their families sometimes have to wait decades before they even see a tiny glimmer of hope in their battle for justice. The Jessica Lal trial, which was believed by many to be a clear open-and-shut case, became a collective banner to rally behind and led to large-scale public protests.

---

[69]H.C. Black, *Black's Law Dictionary (Second Edition)*, The Lawbook Exchange.

India's private news channels also decided to take on the role of the public conscience and began to rally support for the cause. There were media-led nationwide campaigns using mobile technology, and information regarding the Jessica Lal case spread across most of urban India like wildfire. The 24-hour news channel, which was then a recent phenomenon in India, came of age. NDTV organized an SMS campaign and managed to garner two lakh text messages petitioning for a new trial. A candlelight vigil at Delhi's India Gate was also held. Photographs of protestors at the vigil demanding a fresh trial would become one of the most iconic images of twenty-first-century India. The pictures featured on the front pages of newspapers across the nation and the world.

The coordination of the protests was greatly influenced by popular cinema and media—the national English media played a leading role in organizing the protests and making the case a national issue of justice and reform, while the smash-hit Bollywood movie *Rang De Basanti* inspired the middle class to support a serious social issue and join the candlelight vigil. The public outcry came to represent a new front in India's simmering class war, where it was thought the rich and powerful could get away with crime while the poor and the middle class were vulnerable to what was perceived as India's failing judicial and police system.

The protests led to the Delhi police filing an appeal to review the acquittal before the Delhi High Court. Meanwhile, Manu Sharma retained India's most high-profile defence lawyer, Ram Jethmalani, who, at the outset, argued that there was little to merit a retrial, but his argument was rejected by the High Court.

ROLE OF THE MEDIA

As soon as the retrial was admitted, India's news media began discussing the case live on air and various experts were called in to offer their opinions. The Indian media, since independence, has been reserved when it comes to the coverage of judicial proceedings, treating them with an air of reverence. At least on paper, Indians have staunchly believed that the independent judiciary is the guardian of the rights of the common man. The Supreme Court's pronouncements have always been treated with respect and faith in India. However, with this case, the gloves seemed to have come off and it was tried as much in the media as it was in courtrooms. The public seemed to be baying for blood, and news coverage only played on their sentiments. So much so that in a primetime interview on national television with Ram Jethmalani, counsel for the accused, a news anchor asked him why he would agree to defend a guilty person. When Ram Jethmalani referred to the fact that Manu Sharma was to be presumed innocent until proven guilty, this correct legal assertion was met with mockery and scorn.

If India's news channels were working overtime to maintain public opinion at a fever pitch, India's print media was working behind the scenes trying to dig up what it could. *Tehelka* broke a sensational news story in September that year. A sting operation had revealed that witnesses of Jessica Lal's murder had been bribed in exchange for modifying their testimonies. Venod Sharma, a Congress minister, was implicated in the grand exposé and was forced to resign from his place in the Haryana cabinet.

THE HIGH COURT

One of the key witnesses in the case was actor Shayan Munshi. He claimed that he had narrated the story to the police in English and they had written it down Hindi. Munshi claimed that he could not speak Hindi and that he had been unaware of the contents of the statement he had signed at the police station. He told the trial court that though the statement said that he could identify the killer, in truth, he had no idea who had shot Jessica. It must be noted that Shayan was educated in Kolkata and had acted in a moderately popular Hindi movie, *Jhankar Beats*, prior to the incident. In the light of such circumstances, his assertion that he did not understand Hindi was difficult to reconcile with common sense.

The Delhi High Court rejected his argument. It stated that given these circumstances, more reliance should have been placed on the testimony of Malini and Bina Ramani. The court went on to say that Munshi's story of two gunmen was a clear and apparent 'lie'. On 15 December 2006, the court convicted Manu Sharma of the murder of Jessica Lal and sentenced him to imprisonment for life. The prosecution had sought the death penalty but the court said that the case was not deserving of such as the murder, though intentional, was not pre-meditated, and therefore did not fit into the 'rarest of rare' criteria for the awarding of the death penalty. The nation rejoiced, and celebrations spilled out of Delhi's news studios.

Manu Sharma, through his counsel, appealed to the Supreme Court saying that he had not received a fair trial. The trial, he claimed, had been coloured by the media and the conviction deserved to be set aside. On 19 April 2010, the Supreme Court confirmed the verdict of the Delhi High Court and refused to set aside the conviction. Manu Sharma would go down now, officially, as the one who murdered Jessica Lal.

AFTERMATH

Manu Sharma is currently serving his life sentence at Delhi's Tihar Jail. In 2009, he was let out on parole and was caught in a scuffle with the son of a police commissioner at a Delhi nightclub. A prisoner can be allowed out of jail for some time if the governor is presented with an adequate reason to do so. The first time, Manu Sharma was let out to perform the last rites of his grandmother and attend to his ailing mother. Further, he asked to be released temporarily to look after the failing family business. Given that his grandmother had died in 2008 and not in 2009, and that his mother was seen at many social functions, his parole did raise a few eyebrows. When he was found partying at a nightclub, it was revoked immediately. In November 2011, he was paroled again so that he could attend the marriage of his younger brother.

The case was the basis for a major Bollywood movie called *No One Killed Jessica*. Shayan Munshi and the other hostile witnesses also face perjury charges and those cases are presently pending before court.

AUTHORS' NOTE

The impact of the Jessica Lal case was multi-fold. On one level, it showed how the media could shape and mould public opinion in India, something that it had not done before. A sustained media campaign had been conducted for a public cause, a relatively new phenomenon in India. Today it has become commonplace, but this case marked the coming of age moment for India's 24-hour news media. Photographs and commentary were beamed into living rooms across the country, and the media was instrument in building up public opinion against the judicial process and Manu Sharma.

The case also drew attention to the fact that the Indian middle class finally felt powerful enough to claim a valid stake in the system. The middle class had been becoming increasingly frustrated with the Indian justice system and demanded the case to be reopened. The fact that the courts complied shows that India's growing middle class was also growing more powerful.

For the first time, the judicial system was inspected and scrutinized by the public, and was found wanting. Manu Sharma was convicted, after all his appeals, in the year 2010, eleven years after the incident. India's judicial system was found slow, and after this case, fast-track courts for high-profile cases have become more common.

The case also highlighted how a person could be found guilty in the court of public opinion before they were found guilty in a court of law. It shows that while the judicial system is susceptible to the rich and powerful, it may also be susceptible to the influence of public opinion. The integrity of the judicial process seemed to shift from one extreme to another in this case, rather than appearing fair to all parties concerned. To the neutral observer the case revealed the fact that India's criminal justice system was in desperate need of reform. The process seemed to either bend to the whims of the rich or to the demands of the mobs and seldom can a trial like that of the murder of Jessica Lal be considered fair to any of the parties involved.

If a judicial process is to work, its integrity must be held paramount, for without this integrity, the process becomes meaningless. If the process is found to pander to either the rich or the powerful or even to public opinion, the trial ceases to be a fair trial. Since the Supreme Court did its job in weighing the evidence fairly, as did the High Court, perhaps the process is not vulnerable at the level of the judges. However, it is vulnerable on the level of the lowest investigating officers, who can change the course of a proceeding by operating under bias during the very early and critical stages.

One cannot help but ask—was there enough evidence to convict Manu Sharma in the High Court, and why was the conviction not passed in the trial court in the first place? Did the prosecution need a wake-up call in order to do its job and put a murderer behind bars? Also, if the case had failed at the trial court level, should that not create room for reasonable doubt, even if the lack of evidence was because of sloppy prosecution, and not innocence? This case is one that seems symptomatic of the failing governmental and administrative machinery in India and reflects the requirement of some broader corrective action that needs to be taken if the system is to survive.

NAINA SAHNI:
THE TANDOOR MURDER

'Murder is not about lust and it's not about violence. It's about possession. When you feel the last breath of life coming out of the woman, you look into her eyes. At the point, it's being God.'

—Ted Bundy

MURDER IS PROBABLY one of the oldest crimes in the history of the human race. If we are to go by the Bible, murder was the first crime committed. But crimes happen every day in India, and murder is no more a shocking crime worthy of making it to the front page of the newspaper. If a crime has to make the front page nowadays, it must be vicious, it must be out of the blue, and it must be so horrendous that it would give readers nightmares. Such a crime was the murder of Naina Sahni.

BACKGROUND

Naina and Matloob met in the year 1984, while both of them were members of the Delhi University Students Union, and fell in love. However, they decided not to marry each other as they were from different religions and their families would not have agreed. Matloob married a girl from his own community in 1988, but he and Naina kept in touch and remained friends. In the meantime, Naina met Sushil, a young politician. Sushil had always been suspicious of Naina's friendship with Matloob, given their history. After Sushil proposed to Naina, she asked Matloob if he thought Sushil was a good man. Matloob replied in the negative, telling her that he had heard bad things about Sushil. When confronted, Sushil dismissed these allegations as mere jealousy of his success. In 1992, Naina informed Matloob of her marriage to Sushil and also told him that she had been open to Sushil about her past. Six months later, she called Matloob to say that Sushil was not a good person and he had been physically abusing her. Around that time, Sushil began to suspect that Naina and Matloob were having an affair. Sushil was worried that such a scandal in his personal life would ruin his promising political career.

THE INCIDENT

On the night of 2 July 1995, in a restaurant called Bagiya on Ashoka Road, Delhi, a woman called Anaroo screamed, 'Hotel mein aag lagi hai!' (The hotel is on fire!). The hue and cry was heard by a nearby police patrol. The police reached the restaurant and called for backup. Since the smoke was rising in great bellows, the police entered the hotel's barbeque area to investigate. There they found a man named Keshav putting wood and oil into a tandoor. When questioned, Keshav replied that he was a worker of the Congress party and that they were burning old campaign posters and pamphlets. The police noticed human body parts among the flames, and after inspecting the fire, found the charred remains of a woman, her bones partly burned, in a corner. Next to the tandoor they found a large polythene sheet. The sheet had blood stains on it. Upon medical examination of the body, it was found that the face was charred with both eyelids and eyeballs destroyed; the ears, nose and lips were also charred, the teeth were exposed and studded with soot, and other natural orifices were studded with soot particles. The body therefore could not be identified.

After a tip-off from the security guard, a hunt was launched for Sushil Sharma, who was by then a leader of the Congress party. Sushil was nowhere to be found and arrest warrants had to be procured to arrest him. The police investigated the flat he shared with his wife, Naina Sahni. Both of them were not found in the flat. They did find bloodstains, bullet shells, a bullet hole near the air conditioner and photos of Sushil and Naina. The suspicion then arose that the charred body could have been that of Naina. Matloob Karim, who was also a Congress party worker, and who claimed he was very close to Naina, later identified the body.

The murder emerged to be, as is the case of many murders, a crime of passion. Sushil was convinced that Naina was having an affair with Matloob and one day, he walked in on her, talking on the phone to Matloob and drinking alcohol. He had become enraged and had murdered her. He had been accusing her of having an affair with Matloob for a long time prior to the crime, but on 2 July 1995, he acted in the heat of passion and murdered his wife. He then called his friend and told him about it and so began a cat-and-mouse chase with the police. He was finally apprehended in Bengaluru and taken into custody.

The post-mortem examination found metallic shrapnel in Naina's skull. It was also found that the bullets matched the bullet holes and shells found in the flat. On basis of this, the police charged Sushil with the murder of Naina, and charged

Keshav as an accomplice. They were brought to trial and were tried before the sessions court in Delhi.

THE TRIAL

Since there were no eyewitnesses or documentary evidence to be relied upon as first-hand evidence of the murder, the prosecution had to rely on circumstantial evidence to create a sequence of events based on their best guess of what had happened. The twist came when Sushil denied ever being married to Naina. He even stated that he did not live in the flat. So, it had to be proved first that he was living with Naina, married or not. A parade of witnesses testified before the sessions court that they had seen Sushil and Naina living in the flat together and that they had all known them as husband and wife. Further, Matloob stated that Naina had told him that they had been married in secret.

The clinching evidence for the crime was the ballistics and post-mortem reports. The post-mortem concluded that she had died of head trauma and that there were bullets found in the skull. The ballistics report confirmed that the bullets were fired from the same .22 calibre gun that Sushil had been found carrying in Bengaluru at the time of his arrest. The court found Sushil guilty of Naina's murder since the body, the murder weapon and the motive for the murder were all present.[70]

Further circumstantial evidence also established the overall depravity of the murder. After murdering Naina, Sushil had chopped her body up, put it in a polythene bag and had then attempted to burn the body in a tandoor. The cool and

---

[70]*State vs. Sushil Sharma* (2007 CriLJ 4008).

calculating way in which Sushil had attempted to destroy the body and the sheer depravity of the act was established. Killing in the heat of passion is one thing, but committing murder and immediately attempting to cover up the crime in a cool-headed, calculating way showed that inside the accused's unassuming appearance, beat the heart of a menacing killer.

SENTENCING

Sentencing a man for a crime takes a great measure of skill and understanding. In India, a person is not given a death sentence when they murder someone; the usual rule is to lock them up for life. Murderers who practise exceptional depravity are the ones who are hanged. Naina was a helpless woman—she lived with her husband who refused to acknowledge her to the world. He used to abuse her. When he suspected an affair, he did not fear for his marriage, but feared for his political career being tainted by scandal. He shot her in the head more than once, and in completely cold blood, chopped her body up and attempted to burn it in a barbeque where people's food is prepared. The court was disgusted by the idea that Sushil could think that he could get away with it merely because he had political power. Many high-profile criminals, especially the ones with political power, often use their power to claim immunity, something that is accessible to few. In light of this, the court saw it fit that the accused should be put to death for this heinous act; a murderer who had conducted an act of such depravity was not worthy of access to human life. Keshav was sentenced to seven years of imprisonment for attempting to conceal evidence.

APPEAL

When a trial court in India pronounces a death sentence, the case is automatically sent to the High Court for review. The Delhi High Court upheld the conviction and the sentence, finding no merit in Sushil's appeal. The court stated:

> 'In the present case, we find that the act of the appellant reflects extreme depravity. The gruesome manner in which the appellant had killed Naina Sahni and dealt with her body must have shocked the conscience of the community at large and we unhesitatingly say that the abhorrent act of the appellant has definitely shocked our judicial conscience also.[71]'

The court also commented on Sushil's lust for power:

> 'People like the appellant who are power drunk and have no value for human life are definitely a menace to the society at large and deserve no mercy. As a leader of the youth, the appellant should have shown courage in some other field in place of butchery. The act of the appellant is so abhorrent and dastardly that in case the death penalty is not awarded to him, it would be a mockery of justice, and the conscience of the society at large would be shocked.[72]'

The court confirmed the death sentence and determined that Sushil Sharma would face the noose.

---

[71]*State vs. Sushil Sharma*, 2007 CriLJ 4008.
[72]*State vs. Sushil Sharma*, 2007 CriLJ 4008.

THE SUPREME COURT

The Supreme Court, on hearing the appeal, upheld Sushil's conviction.[73] The Supreme Court, however, commuted the death sentence to life imprisonment. It stated that, in its opinion, Sushil was not beyond reform. The Supreme Court, while recording its reasons for mitigating the sentence, stated:

> 'Murder was the outcome of a strained personal relationship. It was not an offence against the society. The appellant has no criminal antecedents. He is not a confirmed criminal and no evidence is led by the State to indicate that he is likely to revert to such crimes in future. It is, therefore, not possible in the facts of the case to say that there is no chance of the appellant being reformed and rehabilitated. We do not think that that option is closed. Though it may not be strictly relevant, we may mention that the appellant is the only son of his parents, who are old and infirm. As of today, the appellant has spent more than 10 years in death cell. **Undoubtedly, the offence is brutal but the brutality alone would not justify death sentence in this case.** The above mitigating circumstances persuade us to commute the death sentence to life imprisonment.'[74]

The Supreme Court pointed out that murders by themselves are brutal, and brutality was insufficient grounds for a case to qualify for the death penalty. The Supreme Court also noted that the murder in question was caused by bullet injuries and that the brutality was only towards the corpse.

---

[73]*Sushil Sharma vs. State (NCT) of Delhi*, (2014) 4 SCC 317.
[74]*Sushil Sharma vs. State (NCT) of Delhi*, (2014) 4 SCC 317.

AUTHORS' NOTE

Sushil Sharma was a man of power and he believed that it offered him protection—he misused his power to attempt to escape the repercussions of the murder of someone whom he had the duty to protect. In India, a politically powerful person seldom faces justice. In this case, however, the political establishment abandoned him. The law tries to preserve a social order where society exists as a whole, but a man who commits such a heinous crime in order to further his own lust of power is assumed to be beyond societal rehabilitation. A cold jail cell is all that Sushil deserved, and got.

Acts of depravity are few in society and most human beings are not capable of them. But in this case, a promising political career had made a man drunk on power, and it had convinced him to see his wife as an obstacle to his political progress rather than as a partner in life. He decided that it would be best to get rid of her. He had been so power drunk that he believed that he could get away with it. It is a scary thought that a human psyche can be capable of such violence and depravity, and values conditioned from childhood can so easily be replaced with a lust for power.

Further, it brings to light the consequences of living in a society where choices are often dictated by religion. Matloob and Naina loved each other. It was only their differing religious affiliations that made them decide to abandon the idea of getting married, leading to the eventual union between Naina and Sushil. Perhaps, if times had been different, and if Naina could have married the man she truly loved, she would have still been alive. There are consequences to all actions and it is but one grain of sand that leads to a landslide. It can be argued that Naina was a victim of a society which is sharply divided on religious lines. It could also be a mere coincidence that Sushil turned out to be a cold-blooded murderer. One can speculate, but the pen that writes the course of humanity seldom adheres to the laws of reason.

THE TELGI STAMP PAPER SCAM

'A man who has never gone to school may steal a freight car; but if he has a university education, he may steal the whole railroad.'

—Theodore Roosevelt

SCAMS OFTEN EXPOSE the weakness of a system. Just like a hacker who manipulates the weakness of a website or a software, a scam artist finds weaknesses in real-life systems and exploits them. However, it takes a scam artist with a special flair to pull off a scam so outrageous that it catches the public eye. When it is finally exposed, the framers and keepers of the system are supposed to introspect and create safeguards to prevent more such scams from occurring. But in a country like India, measures are rarely taken to close the loopholes.

WHO WAS TELGI?

Abdul Karim Telgi, born in 1961, was the second son of a railway employee from Belgaum, Karnataka. His father died when he was young and he worked his way through his English-medium school by selling vegetables on trains. He later immigrated to the Middle East to earn more money, as many young men, back then and today, are wont to do. Little is known about the time

Abdul spent in the Gulf, but he came back to India and settled down in its largest metropolis, Mumbai. The rags-to-riches story began with the oldest trick in the book—forgery.

Forgery, the more formal term for it being counterfeiting, is the process of creating fake documents. For a long time it was an offence punishable by death under the law of England. Today, the law is a lot less harsh for forgery, but creating a copy of a government document is not an inexpensive and easy task either. Each government seal on a document comes with its own complicated pictograms and in-built anti-counterfeiting measures. To understand the protection measures that the government uses to prevent its documents from being forged, simply look at the average currency note and check the amount of copy-protection features involved. Many machines, including scanners and printers, are programmed to recognize these documents and not copy them. Forgery today, as it did in the olden days, requires a certain skill set—it is almost an artistic endeavour, where one tries to create a replica from the original. The replica cannot be perfect, but the errors in the forged replica need to be so minute that to an average eye, and sometimes even to a trained one, they may not be apparently visible.

Telgi's career as a forger began with forging passports. This had almost become a cottage industry in India. Today, it is harder to forge a passport due to computerization and the move towards biometric passport systems, but back during the roaring 1980s, passports were hard to obtain and easy to forge. An experienced forger who was willing to forge a travel document could make good money. However, in the 1980s, the demand for passports was not very high. International travel was expensive and a majority of those who could afford it could also afford the bribes required to speed up the passport process; thereby, they usually did not need the black market to procure a passport. The real money for the forger lay in the forging of stamp paper.

STAMP PAPER SCAM

Stamp duty is a duty payable to the government on certain transactions conducted within a particular territory. The name though, is a misnomer—it is actually simply just a tax on transactions. It is levied on different transactions depending on their value and size and is one of the primary sources of revenue for many state governments. The payment of the duty is evidenced by a stamp on the document which legitimizes the transaction. For example, when a property is leased out, the lease is a transaction and the lease agreement serves as its evidence. A government stamp on the lease document is evidence that the duty payable to the government has been paid, and therefore, the transaction is valid and registered with the government. The stamp duty had been one of the primary means of revenue generation in India since the British rule till today. Stamp papers are foolscap sheets of paper with pre-fixed revenue stamps on them. Purchase of stamp papers ensures that the duties enter the coffers of the government. It is an easy method of collecting government duties, and the parties involved are not required to go to a government office to pay the tax. However, the system is old and archaic, and is therefore prone to weakness. It was this weakness that a scam artist from Belgaum was able to exploit. This was one of the biggest scams in Indian history and caused intense embarrassment to the government.

Abdul Karim Telgi decided that one of the quickest and most lucrative ways to make money would be by creating counterfeit stamp paper, which could later be sold and the revenue, instead of going to the government, would go directly into his pocket. The scam would be hard to execute; government stamp papers are printed using expensive machinery and access to this machinery is controlled and restricted. Further, once the fake documents are printed, the fake stamp paper needs to infiltrate the legitimate supply channels. The second part would not be as difficult, as many businesses and individuals procured their stamp papers from touts who would buy the stamp paper and then sell the paper at a premium. These touts formed an essential part of Telgi's network. But acquiring the machinery to print the papers required a large-scale covert operation. However, everything is available for a price. The right sum of money, paid to the right person and at the right time, could ensure the right result. Telgi knew this only too well, given his previous experience with forging passports. Relying on the wealth of his previous scam experience, Telgi soon acquired the necessary machinery and began printing stamp paper.

The counterfeit stamp paper soon flooded the Indian market and numerous transactions were done using these fake papers. The bribes paid to keep the scam under wraps were also enormous. A telling example was that of additional inspector Dilip Kamath—his salary was a mere ₹9,000 a month, but when the special investigation team looked into his assets, they were found to be in excess of ₹100 crore. The scam was huge and was estimated to be worth around ₹26,000–36,000 crore. It remained hidden because of the large bribes that were paid to ensure that various 'favours' were given to Telgi to help him keep it under wraps.

THE SCAM BREAKS

In 2000, the Karnataka police arrested two persons who were caught carrying fake stamp papers. This opened up an investigation which leads to the recovery of more such forged papers worth around ₹9 crore. Telgi's name surfaced in the investigation and he was arrested in Rajasthan by the Karnataka police and was lodged in the central jail in Bengaluru. This was not the end of it—Telgi's spirit of entrepreneurship continued to flourish in jail. He bribed police officers and other personnel to enable him to stay in an air-conditioned hotel room and continue his activity. He was permitted unlimited phone calls and the enterprise continued while Telgi was technically behind bars. Little did he know that the Karnataka police were secretly tapping his phone, and as a result, there were over 1,200 hours of taped conversation, which implicated the big and powerful as being part of the scam. Investigations were conducted across the country. Telgi was once again apprehended and jailed. Around the same time, his health began to take a turn for the worse. He was diagnosed with AIDS; as a result, his falling health was used as a mitigating circumstance by his lawyers to ensure that he never had to leave the Bengaluru jail. Instead, he made most of his trial appearances via video conference.

NARCO ANALYSIS

There is a Latin phrase, *in vino veritas,* which roughly translates to, in wine there is truth. This is a known fact—when a person is intoxicated and he cannot consciously lie anymore, there is a good chance that he will reveal the truth. The police use a similar method to obtain information during investigation, called narco analysis. The person being questioned is injected with a chemical that inhibits the sensory part of the brain that allows them to lie, and then an interrogation is conducted. The information from these interrogations often prove crucial to investigations. Narco analysis has always been controversial from a human rights perspective, since it raises the question whether such an investigation violates the rights of the accused. One of the most important rights given to the accused is the right to remain silent and not incriminate himself; there are concerns that narco analysis violates this specific right. In 2010, the Supreme Court held that narco analysis without the consent of the accused is unconstitutional. However this narco analysis was conducted in 2003, before the ruling and was therefore valid.

During the videotaped interview, under influence of the drug, he named Sharad Pawar, the then chief of the National Congress Party (NCP), the former Deputy Chief Minister of Maharashtra, Chhagan Bhujbal, and the former Karnataka tourism minister Roshan Baig, as being involved in the scam. Investigations were launched into the involvement of these politicians but the results of the investigation were inconclusive.

THE TRIALS

Telgi, in total, faced forty-seven different cases against him in different jurisdictions. His first major conviction was in 2007, where he was sentenced to a period of thirteen years rigorous imprisonment. In 2011, he was further awarded a sentence of ten years by a Pune court in another case. The sentences were to run one after the other. If a person is convicted of multiple crimes and sentenced more than once, they can request that their sentences run concurrently, which means that time served in once sentence can be used as time served in another. If allowed to run concurrently, Telgi would effectively be imprisoned for only thirteen years. But the court refused to allow this due to the gravity of the crime and, therefore, after his first sentence would be completed his second one would begin. Many other cases are still under trial and Telgi was expected to spend the rest of his natural life in jail.

However, his remaining natural life itself looks short, since his condition has been deteriorating rapidly because of AIDS. He has lost of lot of weight and cannot stand on his own and requires assistance to use the bathroom. He is constantly under medication. His poor health may result in many of his trials being cut short and many of the cases and appeals never being resolved, as it was in the case of the other great scam artist in India, Harshad Mehta.

AUTHORS' NOTE

The Telgi scam was certainly one of the biggest scams in the last few decades, and has left a lasting impact on the government and in the minds of the people of the country. Even today, many of the cases related to this scam are pending in courts with different pleas entered in different cases. The Telgi scam has come to symbolize everything that is wrong with the way the Indian dream is pursued by many. The scam artist came from rags and he sought the riches that a very privileged few have in India, and was willing to break the law to get it. It is symptomatic of a society where the gap between the have and have-nots forces the excessively ambitious to resort to any means possible to make it big. The route to wealth by legitimate means was too slow for the young Abdul, as it is for many disgruntled youth in an increasingly alien and modern India.

The spirit of Indian entrepreneurship that drives the great Indian growth story was used to drive the great Indian criminal enterprise. One can only wonder if Telgi's story would have ended differently had the circumstances been different—if he had put his entrepreneurship skills to legitimate business as many have done, would he today be one of India's great businessmen? The scam that he ran required a level of skill that is seldom found in most people.

The scam also exposed many weaknesses in the government machinery. The ease with which stamp paper could be forged forced many state governments to examine the way stamp duty was being collected. To try and plug the loopholes in the system, new innovations were introduced in the form of e-governance. Today, in several states, stamp paper is no longer sold; e-stamp paper has become the norm, which can now be procured from any bank or financial institution authorized to collect money. Once the money is paid at the counter, the stamp paper is printed with a unique code tied to the PAN number of the buyer. Each sheet of stamp paper is unique and tied to an individual, reducing the secondary market for it and allowing for more secure stamp duty collection. If it were not for the Telgi scam, the slow pace of government-led infrastructure change in India would have ensured that these innovations would not have come into force. The scam also exposed the extent of corruption within the system and how vulnerable public servants at all levels are to bribery. While problems like corruption cannot be easily wished away, implementing modern methods to collect stamp duty would certainly prevent future scams following the same modus operandi.

THE JAIN HAWALA CASE

'The only way to stop the flow of this dirty money is to get tough on the bankers who help mask and transfer it around the world. Banks themselves don't launder money, after all; people do.'

— Robert Mazur, *The New York Times*

MONEY, AS MANY say, is fungible. It has a tendency to move unnoticed and faster compared to anything else manmade. From the time of the ancient civilizations, the Indian subcontinent has been at the forefront of finance with what is considered to be the first financial instrument (negotiable instrument), the *hundi*. Indians traders used promissory notes and negotiable instruments like the *hundi* in ingenious ways to conduct business operations across the vast subcontinent and with Mesopotamia and Egypt in the west and with China in the east. Over centuries, governments have tried their best to curb the flow of such funds, yet governments can also be swayed by a certain group's ability to mobilize money. In modern times, J.P. Morgan was called around 1912 to depose before the House Committee of the US Senate to assure the government of his ability to raise and mobilize funds for US' allies. A few decades earlier, Prescott Bush and many other legendary corporations have been known to have aided the Nazi regime by helping to move the Nazi gold confiscated through questionable means from the Jews fleeing from Germany. Time and again, money finds a way to move beyond the government radar.[75]

One of the many such popular routes to divert money from official circulation and under the government radar is called hawala. It is one of the most ancient systems of money transfer and works just like some postal money transfer systems or wire transfer agencies. However, in the hawala system, there is hardly any written record or settlement of transactions. Before we begin discussing one of the greatest scams of the 1990s, it is essential to first understand how hawala works.

WHAT IS HAWALA?

Say X is a person in India who wants to give money to Y in Kabul. X could go to his bank and transfer the money via a bank transfer, but this would mean two things:

- Paying a commission on the transfer; and
- Creating a legal record that such a transfer existed.

Perhaps X wants to avoid creating any records, because that would mean he could get taxed. So X approaches a hawala broker A and gives him the money along with a 'password'. The password usually tends to be a unique number on a currency note. A contacts a hawala broker in Kabul, B, and tells him

---

[75]For further reading on monetary mobility and the creation of black money, along with recent governmental and international efforts to address these issues, those interested may refer to *Capitalism's Achilles Heel: Dirty Money and How to Renew the Free Market System* by Raymond W. Baker, published by John Wiley and Sons Inc.

the secret password and that he has received the money. In the meantime, X gives Y the password. Y presents the password to B and collects the money. Therefore, instantaneously, the money has been transferred from X to Y. A and B earn a commission for their services. A and B would later settle accounts in their own fashion, either in the form of goods, or sometimes as an actual cash transfer.

The interesting feature of this system is that the money that X had given Y never actually left India nor was it converted into foreign exchange before it was transferred. In contrast, if they had conducted a bank transfer, the rupee would first be converted into a reserve currency (USD, JPY, GBP or EUR) in India, then the reserve currency amount would be transferred to the bank in Kabul, who would then convert it into the local currency there. This involves numerous records and commissions which some businessmen prefer to avoid. There is only one problem with a hawala transfer—it is illegal. However, in spite of that, a full-fledged parallel underground system of money transfer through hawala has thrived in India and continues to do so.

Why did this seemingly harmless business practice acquire such notoriety? It's the most efficient way to move black money around as such kind of money is seldom legally declared. Further, as in the case of the Jain hawala scam, it could be used in terrorist financing.

THE SCANDAL

In 1991, the Income Tax Department raided the premises of the Jain brothers and found diaries in which there were clear records of hawala transactions. This was after the arrest of two Kashmiri militants. It was discovered that they were being funded via hawala channels, which were traced back to the Jain brothers—S.K. Jain, N.K. Jain and B.R. Jain. The brothers had maintained a diary of accounts for their personal use, which was seized. The diary allegedly included details of payments made to significant politicians as bribes for awarding the brothers favourable contracts, in addition to records of most of their hawala transactions. The Jain brothers, being businessmen, perhaps thought it prudent to keep books of accounts to ensure that their money, even if it is black money, was being spent in an efficient and accountable manner.

In August 1991, a journalist, Vineet Narain, in his video cassette news series called *Kalachakra*, broke the news of the scam. He claimed that the hawala money were being used to fund mujahideen in Jammu & Kashmir and such transactions were a danger to national security. The Central Board of Film Censors (CBFC), India's film censorship watchdog, prevented it from being exhibited to the public. Vineet appealed against this order. The Censor Tribunal reversed it, saying that the film is investigative journalism and deserves to be protected under the guarantee of free speech and allowed for it to be exhibited. The tribunal went on to state that in order for a democratic society to thrive, the probity of public life was essential, and therefore the documentary must be screened.

Many leading politicians were implicated in the scam. Most notable among them was L.K. Advani, senior leader of the BJP, and the man who would later become the Deputy Prime Minister of India. Also implicated was Arjun Singh, a former Chief Minister of Madhya Pradesh (under whose tenure the Bhopal Gas Tragedy took place), and who would later become union HRD minister. The late V.C. Shukla, who had served as the information and broadcasting minister at the union cabinet during the Emergency and the dark days of suspended free speech, was also implicated. The news of the scam broke in 1994 and the scandal broke across political lines and implicated politicians across the spectrum. In 1994, a PIL was filed before the Supreme Court by Vineet, asking it to direct the CBI to investigate the scam. In 1996, a large number of sitting cabinet ministers and members of parliament were charge-sheeted with being involved in the crime. The others who were charge-sheeted included Chief Ministers and governors. It was as though the entire political class in India was being put on trial.

The Kashmiris involved were tried under the draconian Terrorist and Disruptive Activities Act (TADA) and were quickly convicted. The politicians, however, were tried under the much softer Prevention of Corruption Act even though the scam linked the politicians to financing terrorism. In total, the scam involved around USD 18 million worth of money laundering via illegitimate banking channels and was one of the biggest scams of that time.

UNDUE INFLUENCE

Indians tend to believe that investigations and trials that involve powerful politicians or influential members of society are almost always affected by intimidation and bribery at the witness or even judicial level. While modern technology and an active media have resulted in far greater information symmetry, reducing the possibility of such judicial tampering today, it must be kept in mind that this case was being investigated in a politically unstable and recently liberalized India. In 1997, Vineet Narain wrote to the Chief Justice of India (CJI) saying that the CBI and other authorities were trying to hush up the scandal, and in late 1997,

Justice Verma and Justice S.C. Sen declared in open court that they were under pressure to keep silent. An important figure in this process was a man called Dr Jolly Bansal, a close associate of the Jain brothers, who was in charge of 'managing' the entire judicial process. In 1998, in a sworn affidavit and before the media, Dr Jolly confessed that he was trying to influence the judges in the case. Vineet Narain then wrote to the Attorney General of India asking for suitable action to be taken against Bansal. Till date, there is no information of any action taken against him despite the confession.

EVIDENCE AND RELATED LAWS

Before a court can legitimize a finding as a fact, it must examine the evidence adduced. Evidence is information, interpreted either from objects or witnesses, that a court shall take into account before concluding that a fact exists. The prosecution's primary proof in this case was the diaries that the brothers maintained, which implicated the accused. However, can these diaries be admitted as evidence? The law does provide for the admission of 'books of account' of a company as evidence if the company is subject to legal proceedings. In this case, the primary question was whether the diaries constituted books of account for the purpose of evidence law. And if they did, then how much reliance could be placed on them.

This question was subject to much contemplation and the Supreme Court finally settled the matter and stated that the diaries could be admitted as evidence, but they could not be used as primary evidence. This meant that the prosecution could rely on the diaries, but could not solely rely on them. They could use the diaries to back up other evidence, but could not bank on the diaries as the principal proof.

PUBLIC SERVANTS

There was another interesting question that arose in the Jain hawala scam cases: is a sitting member of parliament a public servant? This was an important question since the Prevention of Corruption Act applied only to 'public servants' and not to all employees of the government. So, if bribes were indeed paid, a case could be made out under the act only if the accused were actually public servants. Another interesting aspect is that government sanction is required prior to prosecuting a public servant. This is common in most democracies, though it may not make sense on the face of it. A public servant is a person who works for the government, and the government needs to carry on its governance of the country at all costs, for the alternative would be a state of anarchy, and that state is not beneficial to anyone. The provision that there needs to be prior sanction obtained before prosecuting a public servant exists in order to ensure that the government is not put under risk of disorder. If the sanction is not granted, the government may use its own disciplinary proceedings to reprimand the public servant.

In 1998, the Supreme Court, in the previously discussed Narasimha Rao, case declared that members of parliament are public servants for the purposes of the Prevention of Corruption Act. This would mean that the Jain brothers could be prosecuted for giving 'illegal gratification', also known as bribes, to members of parliament in order to continue their hawala business. However, due to the course of judicial events listed below, the need for a sanction for prosecution never arose.

VERDICTS AND REASONING[76]

The names of the high-profile politicians involved in the case, namely Sharad Yadav, L.K. Advani, V.C. Shukla and Arjun Singh, were not written down in the diaries and there was little other evidence to prosecute them with. They were not acquitted per se, but it was held by various High Courts and the Supreme Court that there was insufficient evidence to even charge them. They got what is commonly known as a 'quashing order'. Where the prosecution does not seek to serve the interests of justice, the High Court has the discretionary and inherent power under the Code of Criminal Procedure to 'quash' the FIR or the charge sheet. Even when there was some evidence, it was not found to be reliable, and therefore the charge sheets were quashed.

It was a similar story with the Jain brothers; the books of accounts kept by them in their diaries were found to be inconclusive at best and of little probative value. The prosecution was even unable to make out a case for criminal conspiracy (a crime that requires mere proof of intention) let alone offences under the Prevention of Corruption Act. The general public viewed the entire investigation as a great cover-up and some called it India's Watergate scandal.

WHO WATCHES THE WATCHMEN?

The Supreme Court had ordered the CBI to probe into these allegations, and when an investigation so ordered results in no convictions, it is considered quite shocking. The CBI came under public scrutiny and it was thought that the investigative agency

---

[76]*Central Bureau of Investigation vs. V.C. Shukla & Ors*, 1998 AIR 1406.

had made out weak cases because of heavy political pressure. The independence of the CBI was called into question—it is, after all, a government agency and thus prone to the influence of government officials. If it is to function and answer solely to the judiciary, does this not create judicial anarchy? In India, the judges of the Supreme Court are not elected—in fact, no judge in India is directly elected by the people. If the courts are to be the watchmen of the Constitution, then the age-old question arises—who watches the watchmen? If the government is to be the watchman, it must subject itself to public review once every five years as opposed to the Supreme Court, a body that is not democratically accountable under law. These questions arose in 2000, when in an interview with *Zee News*, the former CBI Director, B.R. Lal, who was in charge of the hawala investigations, stated that there was immense political pressure to ensure the prosecution did not succeed. He said that there was sufficient evidence against the accused but there was pressure from 'above' to ensure that the prosecutions were unsuccessful.

Since India has an adversarial system where the prosecution and the defence act independently and do not work with the court, the court merely establishes facts from what is presented before it as evidence. But what is to be done if the prosecution tries to prosecute the very people who control it? The court may sanction and even order that a prosecution be undertaken with regard to the issues at hand; however, this may not always be effective.

Nowhere in the world is the prosecution truly independent from governmental influence. To prosecute or not is a matter of discretion to be handled by the person in charge of prosecutions. In some countries, the prosecution is handled by an independent agency or officer who is elected to perform that role. This officer or agency takes into account political consequences while deciding on a prosecution. India, like most countries, vests the task of prosecution with its government. The government is elected by the people; however, all prosecutions, in some way or the other, cater to the political ambitions of a few. Most people in India considered the failure of the prosecution in this case as a large moral failure, but it wasn't unexpected. When the key players of a system are on trial, the system cannot be expected to sabotage itself by convicting them.

However, the fact that they were charged and the matter went to court shows that a balance can be struck and that all is not lost in this democratic system—at least we know that if a politician makes an error or commits a crime, they will be answerable to someone. If anything, the Jain hawala case give hope to the idea, that maybe in a later day, where there are more moral leaders, a prosecution of those in power can be successful.

AUTHORS' NOTE

L.K. Advani was one of the key accused in these prosecutions and this fact crops up every time someone discusses him. Advani was once the Deputy Prime Minister of India and continues to be a senior political leader. The Jain hawala scam along with the Babri Masjid issue will always find a place in any biography about him and will forever be black spots on his legacy. However, among all the political leaders implicated in the scam, Advani was the only one to have taken a strong stand on his innocence, resigning his position from the parliament and refusing to stand for elections till his name was cleared. Refreshingly, given the standards of our political leadership, he kept his word.

Arjun Singh later went on to become the union minister for human resource development and introduced populist reforms in India's reservation policies as part of the UPA government. The lead defence lawyer in most of the hawala cases, Kapil Sibal, was also a senior member of the UPA government. Sharad Yadav is still a member of parliament and a senior leader of the JD(U) from Bihar. The hawala scam implicated politicians from various parties. The Supreme Court directives on the independence of the CBI are yet to be implemented and the country watches as more scams go on and on. Corruption was, and still is, a way of life in India.

THE RAJIV GANDHI ASSASSINATION

'Assassination is the extreme form of censorship.'

—George Bernard Shaw

WHEN THE WORLD remembers political assassinations, many think of the United States and its history of high-profile assassinations, such as those of Lincoln and Kennedy. However, when one shifts the focus from the first world to countries like India, Pakistan and Bangladesh, political murders are no less common.

Assassinations have been characteristic of South Asian politics since the countries of that region gained independence in the middle of the twentieth century. From M.K. Gandhi, the father of the nation, to Indira Gandhi, a serving Prime Minster, India is not unfamiliar with political assassinations. Most recently, it was the assassination of Rajiv Gandhi, India's former Prime Minister, by the Liberation Tigers of Tamil Eelam (LTTE) in 1991 that shook the country. Rajiv Gandhi became Prime Minister after his mother, Indira, was assassinated by her bodyguards in 1984. In 1991, during an election campaign in Tamil Nadu, Rajiv also became the victim of an assassination. A suicide bombing left him and fourteen others dead. The political background and the aftermath of the assassination serve as a brutal reminder that politics in South Asia can get very violent.

BACKGROUND

On 31 October 1984, Indian Prime Minister, Indira Gandhi, was shot dead by her Sikh bodyguards in retaliation to the Indian Army spilling blood within the Golden Temple in Amritsar and the sweep across Punjab to quell the Khalistan insurgency. Political chaos erupted across the nation and within hours, Rajiv Gandhi was invited by the then president, Zail Singh, to form the government. Rajiv was Indira Gandhi's only surviving son; his brother Sanjay had died a few years earlier in a plane crash. At the time, Rajiv was president of the youth wing of the Congress party, also known as the Youth Congress and was married to an Italian woman, Sonia Maino, later Sonia Gandhi, whom he met while at university. After the anti-Sikh riots in Delhi, Rajiv advised the president of India to dissolve the parliament and call for fresh elections, since the term of the Lok Sabha was about to expire.

He returned to parliament with the largest ever majority in Indian history. In the sympathy wave that swept the nation after Indira's assassination, Congress won 415 out of 533 seats in the Lok Sabha. During Rajiv's term in office, the Indo-Sri Lanka Accord of 1987 was signed. This created the Indian Peace Keeping Force (IPKF), designated to ensure and enforce the ongoing ceasefire in the civil war between Sri Lanka and the LTTE. This could, at best, be described as a tactical victory, since it failed to achieve its objectives. It was also one of the reasons Rajiv Gandhi's government lost the 1989 general elections. Since no party had been able to stake claim to power, two short-lived coalitions, the first led by V.P. Singh, followed by another coalition led by Chandra Shekar, came to power. By 1991, India was facing elections again.

THE ASSASSINATION

On 21 May 1991, Rajiv Gandhi took to the stage at Sriperumbudur, a village on the outskirts of Chennai (then known as Madras). After a series of speeches, he was garlanded by dignitaries. So far, it had seemed like a good day spent campaigning, and seemed as though would extend well into the night, which it did. However, at 10.21 p.m., there was an explosion. A woman had approached to touch Rajiv Gandhi's feet, and while doing so, she had detonated RDX explosives strapped to her body. The assassin, Dhanu, had hidden the explosives in a belt under her dress and as she bent down, she detonated the explosives and just like that, Rajiv was no more. His body was flown by a special plane to Delhi, and on 24 May 1991, he was given a state funeral.

The principal assassin died while carrying out the crime. Later, it was revealed that Dhanu's real name was Thenmozhi Rajaratnam, alias Gayatri. She was part of the LTTE Suicide Squad, a terrorist organization that was responsible for carrying out several suicide bombings between the years 1980 and 2000.

Parallel to these proceedings was the Padmanabha murder case. K. Padmanabha was the general secretary of the Eleam People's Revolutionary Liberation Front (EPRLF), a moderate splinter group of the LTTE, backed by the Indian government, which participated in the democratic process. Padmanabha was assassinated by the LTTE on 19 June 1991 in Chennai.

TADA

The accused were charged with the offence of 'terrorism' under the Terrorist and Disruptive Activities (Prevention) Act of 1985, more popularly known as TADA. The law on criminal procedure in India generally follows the system of substantive due process, i.e., statements made before police officers are generally not admissible, bail is a right and the law tends to frown upon torture. However, with TADA, things work a little differently. Many people called the law draconian when it was passed in 1985. It was the second law in Indian history that required the parliament to pass it in a joint sitting. Highly controversial, TADA was intended to combat terrorism. The law allowed for confessions to the police to be admissible and it further shifted the burden of proof to the accused. According to the Indian criminal justice system, the guilt of the accused must be proved beyond reasonable doubt by the prosecution. Under TADA, this was reversed. It was the job of the accused to prove that they were innocent of the crime. Special TADA courts were set up and one could only appeal their verdicts in the Supreme Court. The case of Rajiv Gandhi's assassination was tried under TADA. This allowed for some interesting conclusions. Along with offences under TADA, the accused were charged with offences under the IPC as well.

INVESTIGATION

A special investigation team of the CBI conducted the investigation. The team was formed within three days of the assassination on 24 May 1991. Meanwhile, the central government set up a commission under Justice Verma of the Supreme Court to investigate the assassination. The Tamil Nadu government also formed a special investigation team to look into the Padmanabha murder. The CBI filed its charge sheet with the special court in Chennai, naming forty-one persons as the accused, twenty-one of whom were Sri Lankan nationals. Number one on the CBI charge sheet was LTTE supremo Prabhakaran. The Tamil Nadu team filed a separate charge sheet naming seventeen accused in the Padmanabha murder case, which interestingly left out the name of Prabhakaran. Before the trial began, the judge of the special court determined that the trial must be videotaped for security purposes and allowed the names of witnesses to be kept confidential as well. The trial took place in a high-security prison in Chennai. The case of Padmanabha's assassination was also tried under TADA. The Tamil Nadu special investigation team handled the case for the prosecution.

THE TRIAL

In 1993, the court framed charges against twenty-six of the accused. The chief accused was Nalini, who was present at the scene of the crime and later confessed her involvement. The court also framed charges against Prabhakaran and extradition requests were sent to the Sri Lankan government. During the course of the trial, over a thousand witnesses were examined by both the prosecution and the defence. Large amounts of documentary and forensic evidence were compiled. In 1997, the court pronounced its verdict in the Padmanabha case, acquitting fifteen of the seventeen accused and convicting the other two. It sentenced them to six and five years of rigorous imprisonment respectively. However, in the Rajiv Gandhi case, the court convicted all twenty-six accused and sentenced them to death.

APPEALS

The verdict of twenty-six death sentences created a legal storm in India. Many in the legal community stated that the trial did not conform to the standards of a fair judicial process. An appeal was made to the Supreme Court, and in 1999, the Supreme Court delivered its verdict.[77] It upheld the death sentences awarded to four of the accused, including Nalini. However, it acquitted the rest. The Supreme Court stated that the assassination of Rajiv Gandhi was not an attempt to overthrow or overawe the government of India. Further, the court stated that the assassination had been in retaliation to the IPKF presence in Sri Lanka and was a direct consequence of an interview given by Rajiv Gandhi where he had stated that if elected he would consider sending the IPKF back to the island country. The court further noted that Rajiv Gandhi had been well aware of the threat and adequate security arrangements were made. However, they seemed to have been throttled by some local Congress leaders for political purposes.

The court also stated that the trial court had erred in its findings, relying on the confessional statements alone as they could have been made under coercion or duress. The court stated that even in cases under TADA a case beyond all reasonable doubt must be made out. As far as twenty-two of the accused were concerned, the court held that such a case had not been made.

The court also concluded that the criminal conspiracy had been hatched in Jaffna, Sri Lanka, and that the assassins had

---

[77]*State of Tamil Nadu through Superintendent of Police, CBI/SIT vs. Nalini & Ors.*, (1999) 5 SCC 253.

made their way to India. They had stayed in India for a prolonged period preparing for the assassination; they had shadowed Rajiv Gandhi and had been looking for an opportunity to go through with their plan. It further went on to say that Rajiv had been the sole target of the assassination plot.

The Supreme Court, however, did confirm the death sentence of Nalini along with the sentences of three others on grounds that there was sufficient evidence to convict them and the case, being an act of terrorism, warranted the death sentence.

AFTERMATH

The four condemned filed mercy petitions before the president of India for commutation of their sentence. Meanwhile, Nalini had a child while she was in prison. The intervention of Sonia Gandhi, Rajiv Gandhi's widow, helped Nalini get clemency. Her sentence was commuted to that of life imprisonment. Meanwhile, the remaining condemned had their petitions pending before the president of India till 2011. Nalini, meanwhile, had applied to the High Court for release in 2010. The state government is allowed to parole a prisoner at its discretion after fourteen years of imprisonment. She argued that she had spent more than fourteen years in prison, but the state government rejected her request of parole. The High Court also denied her request noting the severe nature of the crime.

In 2011, the then president of India, Prathiba Patil, rejected the mercy petitions of the remaining condemned. Ordinarily, after the rejection of a mercy plea, the condemned are usually executed quickly. However, since India is a democracy, it has multiple criteria by which a death sentence can be reviewed. The condemned had spent twelve years waiting for a decision on their mercy petitions. A medical condition known as Death Row Syndrome states that a condemned prisoner undergoes severe trauma waiting for their execution. Since the accused had been on death row for over twelve years, it was argued that executing them after such a long wait would be a violation of their fundamental rights. The Supreme Court in many cases had reversed or commuted such sentences on these grounds. The remaining condemned applied to the Madras High Court for a stay on their execution and as such the stay was granted.

The case is also very polarizing in nature. Tamil Nadu is a key state in India, politically. Further, the Sri Lankan Tamil issue is an extremely sensitive one in Tamil Nadu and is often used to mobilize votes during elections. The state assembly passed a resolution calling for the commutation of the death sentence for the condemned.

AUTHORS' NOTE

There are several important issues to note. The Verma Commission Report critically pointed out that the security arrangements for Rajiv Gandhi had been undermined by other members of the Congress party. The Jain Commission went to the point of indicting the former Chief Minister of Tamil Nadu and DMK party leader, Karunanidhi, in the conspiracy. This caused the collapse of the I.K. Gujaral government in 1998 when the Congress withdrew support on the basis of the allegations.

This case also brought unfavourable attention to the provisions under TADA. The fact that the trial court had sentenced all twenty-six accused to death only to have the Supreme Court largely reverse the verdict shows how TADA is subject to misuse.

The case can also be looked at from the perspective of Tamil nationalism. Ordinarily, in most nations, the assassination of a former Prime Minister evokes national anger. However, in this case, Tamil Nadu was torn between condemning the murder and choosing the Tamil cause over the national cause. Politics in the state continues to be largely influenced by the stand different political parties take on Tamil issues.

The case also created the necessity to discuss the processes by which the death penalty is executed in India. The condemned had their mercy petitions pending for over twelve years before the president. Perhaps the delay had occurred because it was politically convenient. While in the cases of Kasab and Afzal Guru, the execution of the sentence had been swift and quick, in this case, it had been prolonged, perhaps due to political considerations.

The Supreme Court, in a decision on 21 January 2014,[78] held that delays in execution after the rejection of the mercy petition are a violation of the right to life of the convicts. The Supreme Court in this decision stated, 'Like the death sentence is passed lawfully, the execution of the sentence must also be in consonance with the constitutional mandate and not in violation of the constitutional principles.'[79] The condemned in this case, in the light of the Supreme Court's decision on 21 January 2014, can move a writ petition and enforce their right to life under Article 21 of the Constitution of India.

---

[78]*Shatrughan Chauhan & Anr vs. Union of India & Ors.*, (2014) 3 SCC 1.
[79]*Ibid* 262.

CHARLES SOBHRAJ:
THE CAGED SERPENT

'The criminal is the creative artist; the detective only the critic.'

—G.K. Chesterton

TO CALL CHARLES Sobhraj a celebrity criminal would not be a far stretch—only, Sobhraj may object to being called a criminal. In his interviews he has stated repeatedly that he is a wronged individual currently deprived of his human rights in Nepal, where is he serving a sentence of life imprisonment.[80] However, he is undoubtedly one of the most charismatic individuals in recent times to be accused to having committed crimes ranging from murder to robbery. If one has to describe him in the parlance of Bollywood, it can be said that Sobhraj is the quintessential 'jewel thief' or the 'don'—a man who is wanted by the police forces of several nations.

THE INITIAL YEARS

Hotchand Bhawnani Gurmukh Sobhraj, born on 6 April 1944,

---

[80]'The True Charles Sobhraj Story,' *The Times of India: The Crest Edition* (India, 31 July 2010).

was the illegitimate child of a Vietnamese mother and an Indian businessman in Saigon, currently known as Ho Chi Minh City, in Vietnam. Soon after his birth, Sobhraj's father deserted his mother and him and married an Indian woman. When he was four years old, his mother married a French military officer, who adopted Sobhraj.

Sobhraj moved to France with his family in 1953 and was admitted to a school there. However, through his adolescence, he travelled back and forth between France and Indo-China, as he ran away several times in order to reach his biological father. However, he was always sent back and his relationship with his family members always remained tense.

He was imprisoned for the first time in 1963 for auto theft and was incarcerated at a prison in Poissy, near Paris. He, however, charmed and manipulated his way into getting special treatment in the prison from the officials. He befriended Felix d'Escogne, a young Parisian from a wealthy family, who was volunteering at the Poissy prison at that point of time.

After his parole, Sobhraj moved in with d'Escogne and through him was introduced to the high society of Paris. He charmed his way through social gatherings. His exotic background, his intelligence and his ability to smooth talk his way out of any situation earned him many friends. More importantly, it helped him woo Chantal Compagnon, a young Parisian woman from a conservative Catholic family. However, at the same time, Sobhraj was being introduced to the Parisian underworld as well. He started accumulating considerable wealth through a series of scams and burglaries. The 'Dr Jekyll and Mr Hyde' persona of Sobhraj was, however, not known to his friends and benefactors. The two worlds of Sobhraj collided on the day he proposed to Chantal; he was arrested by the police for driving a stolen car and was sentenced to eight months in prison. By this time, d'Escogne realized that Sobhraj is not merely a criminal, but probably a psychopathic one. Felix d'Escogne wrote to the judge suggesting that mandatory psychological counselling be made part of the sentence, and added, 'He exploits 100 percent the weaknesses of those around him [...] He has a small conscience, if any [...] if capable of politeness, but calculatedly so. Impulsive and aggressive [...]'[81]

However, unlike d'Escogne, Chantal was not aware of Sobhraj's true nature. He managed to convince Chantal of his innocence and she, in turn, stood beside him for eight months while Sobhraj was serving his prison term. Sobhraj and Chantal married upon his release from prison, after overcoming the initial disapproval of Chantal's parents. However, Sobhraj continued with his criminal activities. He realized within a short time that it would not take the police long to link him with a series of burglaries that were taking place in several wealthy homes in the area and they would also be able to trace back the bad cheques he had been passing around.

Sobhraj did not waste too much time after this realization. He borrowed a car from none other than d'Escogne, who was by then, back on friendly terms with the couple. Sobhraj took the then pregnant Chantal and travelled through Europe to India. On their way, Sobhraj used fake identity documents and robbed unsuspecting people whom the couple befriended. Sobhraj and Chantal reached Mumbai in 1970, where Chantal gave birth to a baby girl.

It was not difficult for Sobhraj and Chantal to integrate

---

[81]Thomas Thomson, *Sepentine* (New York: Carroll & Graf Publishers, 1979).

into the expatriate population of the city. Sobhraj started his illegal activities in India, with the expat community among his chief clientele. He smuggled stolen foreign cars from abroad, turned them over to the Indian authorities for not having proper documents and bought them back at the auctions. He would sell these foreign cars to the expatriates at a much higher price, which they were willing to pay to own legitimate foreign cars in India, which were hard to get through other channels.

Sobhraj had started gambling heavily around this time as well, and needed more money to cover up his losses. He masterminded a daring armed robbery at a jewellery shop in Hotel Ashoka, in Delhi. However, he failed to escape with the loot as the storekeeper informed the police in time and the authorities sealed the airport. Sobhraj came back to Mumbai and got back to his car theft scam, but soon after, the police arrested him for the jewellery shop robbery.

Sobhraj executed the first of his many famous escapes when he feigned illness and managed to convince the authorities to transfer him to a hospital from the prison. With active help from Chantal, he escaped from the hospital after drugging his guard. However, both of them were arrested and put behind bars by the police. Eventually, both Sobhraj and Chantal were released on bail and fled India along with their daughter.

The couple next moved to Kabul, Afghanistan, where they conned and robbed hippies who had come in from Europe following the hashish trail. However, Sobhraj's luck ran out when he tried to escape Kabul after failing to clear his hotel bills and was arrested. Once in prison, he reenacted his escape trick by getting admitted to a hospital on a feigned illness and drugging his guard. Sobhraj escaped to Iran, leaving behind Chantal and the baby. Chantal left for France intending to leave behind her criminal past and vowing never to meet the man whom she had supported and abetted for so many years. This brought Sobhraj's marriage to an end.

THE RISE OF THE SERPENT

With no family to take care of, Sobhraj travelled to many countries in the next few years, committing petty crimes on his way to support himself. During 1971-72, Sobhraj apparently used more than ten stolen passports to travel to Pakistan, Bulgaria, Italy, Yugoslavia, Iran and other countries. Sobhraj was joined by his younger brother, Andre, in Istanbul, Turkey, where the brothers carried off a few heists before they moved to Greece. Both of them were arrested there for allegedly robbing a jewellery store. Even though Sobhraj planned an identity-switch escape, the plan did not materialize, and ultimately, he escaped in an ambulance after feigning illness. Andre, however, was handed over by Greece to Turkey, where he was put on a trial for thefts, and he was sentenced to imprisonment with hard labour for eighteen years.

Sobhraj moved to Thailand next, where he met Marie-Andrée Leclerc, a French-Canadian tourist. Marie was smitten by the charming Sobhraj, who convinced her to join him in Bangkok. She would go on to become one of his closest confidantes and accomplices. Around the same time, Sobhraj also had dalliances with several women, including a local named May, whom he would refer to as his 'secretary'.

Sobhraj and Marie befriended an Australian couple in Thailand and then poisoned them with coconut milk laced with sedatives, before running off with several thousand dollars and their passports, among other things. Sobhraj then started trying to develop a band of followers or accomplices. His modus operandi for this was to primarily manipulate people by helping them out of difficult situations that he himself would have created in the first place. This godfather-like behaviour reflected his self-obsession and supreme confidence, which would continue to play a role in his future activities.

An instance of this was an incident involving a Frenchman, Domonique Rennelleau. Sobhraj poisoned him without his knowledge, and when Dominique started developing signs of what he felt was dysentery, Sobhraj himself cured and sheltered Dominique at his own home. The unsuspecting Dominique became indebted to Sobhraj for his graciousness. Sobhraj also added two more individuals, Yannick and Jacques, to his coterie. Former French policemen whom Sobhraj and Marie entertained with alcohol, their money and passports were stolen by the couple. Sobhraj then graciously allowed them to stay over at his place till such time as they got new passports, and thus earned their gratitude. The final and most important addition to Sobhraj's band of men was an Indian called Ajay Chowdhury, who soon rose through the ranks to become his lieutenant and co-conspirator.

THE BIKINI KILLER

It is not certain whether Sobhraj had murdered anyone before this time, though the investigating authorities have apprehensions that he did. The first known murders committed by Sobhraj took place in 1975. The victims had spent some time with Sobhraj and his clan before they had been murdered. In the absence of any crucial motive behind these murders, investigating authorities speculate that they were potential recruits who were killed when they did not play along and threatened to expose Sobhraj.

The first victim was a young American woman called Jennie Bollivar (or Teresa Knowlton, according to some accounts), whose bikini-clad body was found in a tidal pool at the Gulf of Thailand. Initially it was believed that it was a case of drowning, but when an autopsy was conducted after months, it was proved that her head had been forcefully held underwater, which lead to her death.

The next victim was Vitali Hakim, a young Sephardic Jew, who had been travelling East to find the meaning of his life. Unfortunately, he had befriended Sobhraj and his accomplices. His terribly burnt body was found on the road to Pattaya. Charmayne Carrou, Hakim's French girlfriend, turned up next looking for him. As she started asking too many questions, Sobhraj and his lieutenant, Chowdhury, decided to hush her up to prevent any exposure. Charmayne's body was found drowned in a pool wearing a bikini, just like Jennie. However, the police could not corelate these crimes immediately. An autopsy conducted much later proved that Charmayne had been strangled before her body was thrown into the water. The murders of both Jennie and Charmayne, who were found wearing bikinis, subsequently earned Sobhraj the nickname of 'bikini killer'.

Around the same time, a young Dutch couple, Henk Bintanja and Cornelia Hemker, were visiting Sobhraj. He had invited them to Thailand after meeting them in Hong Kong. While staying with Sobhraj and his gang, the couple 'mysteriously' fell ill, thanks to some poisoning by Sobhraj. He 'took care' of their passports and valuables when they were recovering. However, one day, Charmayne turned up with her queries about her missing boyfriend, and the Dutch couple were quickly hustled out of the house by Sobhraj and Chowdhury. Their strangled and burnt bodies were found on 16 December 1975 by the authorities.

While it appeared that Chowdhury and Marie were hand in glove with Sobhraj in these crimes, Dominique, Yannick and Jacques were not involved, but by this time, the three of them had become increasingly suspicious of the deaths that had occurred around them.

While the Dutch victims were being identified in Thailand, Sobhraj and Marie quickly fled to Nepal using the passports of the deceased. Sobhraj met another couple in Nepal—Laurent Ormond Carrière and Connie Bronzich (identified as Laddie DuParr and Annabella Tremont in some accounts). While Carrière was a mountaineer from Canada, waiting to climb Mount Everest, Connie Bronzich was an American, who was, like many western tourists to the East at the time, searching for the meaning of life. A few days later, Carrière's slashed and burnt body was found in a field in Nepal, while Connie's body was found nearby with multiple stab wounds on her chest.

Sobhraj used Carrière's passport to fly back to Thailand. While there, he made the startling discovery that the trio— Dominique, Yannick and Jacques—had discovered the gruesome secrets of Sobhraj and had informed the police about the crimes. The police, pressurized by the Dutch embassy on account of the murder of the Dutch couple, had started putting two and two together. Thus, on the run from the Nepalese and the Thai police, Charles, Marie and Chowdhury next fled to Kolkata, India.

Short of money and desperately looking for a clean passport to flee from the authorities, Sobhraj murdered Israeli scholar Avoni Jacob in Kolkata and took his passport, along with $300. He used Jacob's passport to travel to Singapore and back to India, before going to Bangkok again with Marie and Chowdhury.

There, Sobhraj drugged and robbed an American tourist of his passport and money. The trio were picked up by the Thai police in March 1976 for questioning regarding the murders, but were let off soon. The authorities were not keen on a much publicized investigation, which they felt would adversely affect the tourism business of the country, which constituted the bulk of the country's economy.

Even though the Dutch embassy, led by a diplomat, Herman Knippenberg, was pushing the investigation, Sobhraj and his accomplices allegedly managed to bribe the police and flee the country. Herman Knippenberg, in the meantime, gathered evidence and witnesses. Only a month after Sobhraj fled the country, he gained permission from the police to search Sobhraj's apartment, where substantial evidence, including victims' passports, poison, etc., was discovered.

Sobhraj, Marie and Chowdhury were next seen in Malaysia. Chowdhury was sent to procure gems from a mining town there and he was last seen delivering the gems to Sobhraj. After that, Chowdhury seems to have vanished from the face of the earth. It is not conclusively known what happened to him, but it is believed that Sobhraj murdered him and disposed the body somewhere in Malaysia. Marie and Sobhraj then proceeded to Geneva to sell the gems.

THE INDIAN EPISODE

Sobhraj and Marie next shifted their base to Mumbai, where he recruited two westerners, Barbara Smith and Mary Ellen Eather, into his gang. His next victim was a Frenchman named Jean-Luc Solomon. Sobhraj intended to sedate Solomon with the poison and carry out a robbery, but he died in an overdose.

In July 1976, Sobhraj and his gang of three women went to Delhi and set up a new scam. Sobhraj introduced himself as a tour guide to a group of French students who were delighted to find a French-speaking, educated guide in India. Sobhraj gave them some pills, passing them off as anti-dysentery medicines, but were actually meant to sedate them. However, the pills started acting sooner than expected and the students started falling unconscious all over the hotel lobby. Three of the students who realized what had happened and were not affected, caught hold of Sobhraj and handed him over to the Indian police. The police arrested his female companions as well, who divulged a lot of information about Sobhraj's modus operandi.

His arrest roused the interest of international law enforcement agencies. Interpol's dossier on Sobhraj had been growing thicker with his criminal activities across the world and various governments were pushing for his prosecution. He was accused of murders in Thailand and Nepal, jail breaking and other offences in Afghanistan and Greece, along with theft and robbery in Turkey, among other crimes.

The notoriously slow judicial system in India took its time to deal with Sobhraj and his accomplices. Nearly two years passed before they were brought to trial. The living conditions in Indian jails, to put it mildly, are not comparable with their western counterparts even now. And in 1976, before the prison reforms happened in India, and in the middle of the Emergency period, it was quite horrific at the infamous Tihar jail. Political prisoners and criminals were thrown into the same cells, where they counted days till the prosecution would finally start. Torture was used as a method of interrogation or as a means to subdue prisoners considered to be too independent-minded, and was the norm rather than an exception. Spending months or even years in such conditions broke the mind and the physique of many prisoners even before their case was determined one way or the other by a court of law.

Sobhraj, as wily and resourceful as ever, not only managed to survive, but thrived through this period. It was rumoured that he had managed to carry costly gems along with him inside the prison, which he utilized to buy a lavish life within the walls of the jail.

When Sobhraj finally went to trial, the national and international media became obsessed. He too played to the gallery. He hired and fired major criminal lawyers at will. He argued his case himself at the end. However, Sobhraj was convicted on several charges that were brought against him, including attempt to commit robbery, voluntarily causing hurt to commit robbery, culpable homicide not amounting to murder, etc. The prosecution argued for the maximum punishment, maybe even the death sentence, whereas Sobhraj pleaded the judge to take into consideration the time he had already spent in prison. The judge, ultimately convinced, sentenced him to only seven years in prison. He also separately awarded five more years' imprisonment in the case of the abortive attempt to rob the French tourists.

During his stay at Tihar, Sobhraj also tried to alleviate the atrocious living conditions in the prisons and went on a hunger strike. He filed a writ petition against the government on the grounds of inhuman living conditions and torture in prison. A five-judge bench of the Supreme Court passed the now famous judgment, 'Sunil Batra vs. Delhi Administration & Ors' (AIR 1978 SC 1675), condemning the prison conditions.

Sobhraj was described as, 'an under-trial prisoner kept indefinitely under bar fetters, as a security risk [...] sought to be justified by the State under the prison law as a safety procedure'[82]. Justice Krishna Iyer, while delivering an elaborate judgment, quoted extensively from various sources, ranging from American cases to books of jurisprudence, from the autobiography of Pandit Jawaharlal Nehru to books of psychiatry. Justice Iyer, in his inimitable style and passion, upheld the rights of prisoners. He noted that, 'Ever since 6 July 1976, he (Sobhraj) has been kept in bar fetters, duly welded, all these months without respite, through the period of preventive detention and after. We have it on the petitioner's word that no holiday was given to the bar fetter therapy, although the Resident Medical Officer has noted, in the history ticket of the prisoner, entries which are tell-tale [...] Sobraj [sic], in chains, demands constitutional rights for man. For there are several men like him in the same prison, under-trials, indigents, even minors.'

Justice Iyer and his fellow judges reached the conclusion that said, 'We cannot do better than say that the directive principle contained in Article 42 of the Constitution that "The State shall make provision for securing just and humane conditions of work," may benevolently be extended to living conditions in jails.' It was directed that for Sobhraj, 'Such fetters shall forthwith be removed and he will be allowed the freedom of under-trials inside the jail, including locomotion—not if he has already been convicted. In the eventuality of display of violence or escape attempts or credible evidence bringing home such a potential adventure by him, he may be kept under restraint. Irons shall not be forced on him unless the situation is one of emergency leaving no other option and in any case that torture shall not

---

[82]Para 65, *Sunil Batra vs. Delhi administration & Ors.*, AIR 1978 SC 1675.

be applied without compliance with natural justice and other limitations indicated in the judgment.'

This judgment marks a watershed moment for prisoners' rights and prison reforms in India. The under-trials and prisoners currently in Indian prisons can probably thank Charles Sobhraj who played a part in securing the basic rights for the prisoners, irrespective of his personal motives to approach the court.

Now finally convicted, Sobhraj's prison term of twelve years posed another problem for him. The warrant from Thailand, where he was wanted on charges of murder, was valid for twenty years and therefore, there was every possibility that Sobhraj would be deported and tried in Thailand as soon as his prison term ended in India. However, that was not to his liking.

By this time, with money to spare and his immense ability to manoeuvre the people around him, Sobhraj was virtually in control of Tihar prison. After spending about ten years in jail, Sobhraj threw a party inside for his friends and captors. The serpent again played his trusted card of sleeping pills and fled the prison. However, he was soon arrested and put behind bars, this time for a longer period for using sleeping pills and escaping. He later claimed that he had intentionally let himself be arrested so that he could spend more time in Indian jails than be deported anywhere else. Whatever be the objective, Sobhraj spent several more years in Tihar and was released on 17 February 1997. By this time, the case in Thailand had all but collapsed and Sobhraj walked out of prison free.

Sobhraj, on his release, settled in Paris and hired a publicity manager. He began giving interviews for which he charged a high price, and was even in negotiations for book rights. There were talks with a Hindi production house about a potential movie on his life and it was also rumoured that Sobhraj had agreed to sell the rights to his story for a substantial amount.

NOW IN NEPAL

Sobhraj was seen in Kathmandu, Nepal, in September 2003 by a journalist. Based on this information, the Nepalese authorities arrested him from the casino of Yak and Yeti Hotel on the charge of the murders of Laurent Ormond Carrière and Connie Bronzich in 1975. The district court in Kathmandu sentenced him to life imprisonment in August 2004 which, on appeal, was confirmed by the Court of Appeals in 2005. Not to be deterred, Sobhraj approached the Supreme Court of Nepal, which upheld the decision of life imprisonment in July 2010, for the murder of Bronzich.

In the meantime, Sobhraj continued to get international media attention. In 2008, the sixty-four-year-old Sobhraj was said to be engaged to a twenty-year-old woman, Nihita Biswas, who happened to be the daughter of Shakuntala Thapa, Sobhraj's lawyer in Nepal. It was then claimed that Sobhraj married Nihita Biswas on 9 October 2008 in the Kathmandu prison during the occasion of Bada Dashami, a Nepalese festival. However, the prison authorities deny any wedding taking place.

AUTHORS' NOTE

Charles Sobhraj, one of the most enigmatic criminals of modern times, continues to be imprisoned in Nepal. While it is difficult to ascertain whether he is really a psychopath as he is often portrayed to be, it is certain that Sobhraj's crimes have finally caught up with him, even after so many years.

THE NITHARI KILLINGS

'Silence can mock.'

—Thomas Harris, *The Silence of the Lambs*

BIG CITIES TEND to grow suburbs around them. Noida is one such suburb of New Delhi. People have a wide variety of reasons for moving to the suburbs; for some it's the chance to have a quieter life, others enjoy the lush availability of space while raising a family, but for most, it's the security of living in a good neighbourhood without the necessary drawbacks of living in a big city. One of the most notable disadvantages of living in a big city is the high level of crime; suburbs like Noida were places where you could raise families in safety and security. However, the events that took place on 29 December 2006 made suburban families question their sense of security.

On this fateful day, two residents claimed to have found the mortal remains of what appeared to be children in a drain outside their house in Sector D5 of Noida. After finding a decomposing hand, the police were called and suspects were arrested. Within hours, parents living in the area turned up with photos of their children who had been going missing over the course of almost a year, and the police had no clue as to their whereabouts. So when the news about the recovered corpses spread, many anxious parents holding photos surrounded the area around the tank, attempting to identify the remains while each feared the worst.

The residents had been claiming for a while that Surender Koli, the servant of Moninder Singh Pandher, a prominent businessman in the area, was behind the disappearances. The local authorities failed to intervene based on the allegations of residents. Therefore, with the help of the local Residents Welfare Association, they began digging the drain behind Pandher's house in Noida. Initially, the rumour was that the bodies of more than fifteen children had been found; however, the police said that they could not confirm the number of dead bodies without more DNA tests to ascertain the true nature of the crime. They cordoned off and sealed the area and Pandher and his servant were taken into custody.

Meanwhile, news of this discovery spread across the country and the central government decided to enquire if this probe had any inter-state ramifications—if this were true then the CBI would control the investigation. Law and order is exclusively a state subject in India, unless the crime committed has inter-state ramifications. If it does, then the central government could take up the case and ask the CBI to investigate the matter. It was found that this indeed was the case and the CBI was tasked with uncovering the mystery behind the dead bodies.

As these events were unfurling in Noida, the nation welcomed its new year with one of the worst crimes it had ever witnessed. The crimes ranged from the sexual assault of minors, mutilation of their bodies to even allegations of cannibalism, rumours of which surfaced over the course of the investigation. The Nithari killings were one of the worst crimes in Indian history and the public had no intention of letting it go.

THE CRIME

Details about the exact nature of the crimes at Nithari remain sketchy. However, what is known is that there were a wide variety of crimes that were committed. Broadly, the victims had been raped and murdered. The torsos of the children were found missing but DNA tests managed to identify most of the bodies. The crime, as established by the investigation, was as follows: the accused and perpetrator, Surender Koli, used to lure children into the house while his master was away. In the house, he sexually assaulted them, after which he murdered them using knives and other brutal methods.

After this was done, the bodies of the children were mutilated and chopped up into pieces using a meat cleaver and were dumped into the drain near the house. All the victims were minors, except Payal, who was twenty years old according to most news reports. It was alleged that she was a call girl who used to service Pandher. However, even she met the same fate as all of Koli's victims when she was lured in and trapped by him. Initially, there were allegations and rumours that the children had been killed so that their organs could be sold on the black market, but later it was established that the killings were the product of a deviant and sick mind. Koli had attacked the children to fulfil his unnatural gratifications.

The investigation was largely problem-free; Koli and Pandher cooperated with the police throughout the investigation. Koli confessed to most of the crimes, identified most of the victims when given photographs, and led the police to the location of the bodies. Brain-mapping and sodium pentothal (narco analysis) tests were also conducted on both the accused and this allowed the police to gain valuable information regarding the other missing victims. The most shocking development in the Nithari killings was the allegation of cannibalism. It was alleged that the missing body parts were because Koli consumed the flesh of his victims.

THE TRIALS

There were several charges against Koli and Pandher and several trials were running parallel in relation to those charges. In 2009, a special CBI court convicted both Koli and Pandher of rape and murder of fourteen-year-old Rimpa Haldar and sentenced them both to death. Pandher appealed his conviction, which was overturned by the Allahabad High Court, but Koli's conviction stood. His subsequent appeal to the Supreme Court was also dismissed. On 15 February 2011, it adjudicated that the case fell into the category of the rarest of rare, and so merited the application of the death penalty. Koli's mercy petition to the president of India was rejected on 27 July 2014.

A death warrant was issued by the Additional Sessions Judge of Ghaziabad, UP, in Koli's name, since it was contended that he has exhausted all the legal remedies available to him. The warrant was sent to the UP government for making necessary preparations for execution of forty-two-year-old Koli, who has also been sentenced to death in four other cases. While fixing a date of his execution, the learned judge said that Koli appeared to be a serial killer and no mercy could be shown to him.[83]

However, on 2 September 2014, a five-judge bench of the Supreme Court of India passed a landmark judgment in the case

---

[83] *Surender Koli vs. State of Uttar Pradesh,* Review Petition (Criminal) No. 395 of 2014, decided on 8 September 2014.

of *Mohd. Arif vs. Supreme Court of India*[84], where the court held that review petitions of death row convicts need to be heard in open court. It further clarified that the right of a limited oral hearing in review petitions where a death sentence is given, shall be applicable only in pending or future review petitions. The court also stated that in cases where a review petition has already been dismissed but the death sentence has not been executed, the petitioners can apply for the reopening of their petitions within one month from the date of the judgment.

In light of the above pronouncement, as soon as the Ghaziabad court issued the death sentence, Koli immediately approached the Supreme Court for recalling and reviewing of the death warrant issued against him. Considering the urgency of the situation, the division bench of the Supreme Court took up the matter in the middle of the night at 1.30 a.m. on 8 September 2014, as Koli's execution was slated to take place the next morning. The division bench stayed the execution for a week[85].

A three-judge bench of the Supreme Court heard Koli's review petition afresh on 12 September 2014 and stayed the execution further till 29 October 2014. Even as this book went to print, the apex court was set for a detailed hearing of the review petition on 28 October 2014.[86]

While he awaits a review of his petition, Koli has been moved back to Dasna Jail. When his death warrant had been issued,

---

[84]Writ Petition no. 77 of 2014, decided on 2 September 2014.

[85]'Koli gets reprive at the eleventh hour', *The Hindu* (New Delhi, 8 September 2014).

[86]'Nithari Killer's execution stayed till October 29', *The Hindu* (New Delhi, 12 September 2014).

Koli had been moved to Meerat's Chaudhury Charan Singh Jail, since Dasna did not have execution facilities.[87]

Moninder Singh Pandher, his co-accused, was released from Dasna jail after the Allahabad High Court granted him bail on 24 September 2014.[88]

AUTHORS' NOTE

For capital crimes in India, life imprisonment is the rule. The death penalty is the exception to the rule and is handed to the guilty only in the 'rarest of rare' cases, where the crime is heinous, the criminal beyond reform, and only the sentence of death can truly satisfy the collective conscience of the society. Every crime is an attack on society as a whole, but it is only in the case of the most heinous crimes that a violent solution such as the death sentence is granted.

Koli has been convicted for the rape and murder of innocent children. He had taken away their futures after torturing them in his den of horrors. After doing so, he proceeded to mutilate their bodies and allegedly consumed their flesh. In the eyes of society and the court, Koli was an animal incapable of living in civil society.

It is worthwhile to try and understand why a man such as Koli would commit such acts; indeed, why would anyone commit such acts? Koli committed heinous and depraved acts and still has not expressed any remorse for them. The Supreme Court found that he had not expressed any remorse for any of his

---

[87]'Koli back in Ghaziabad jail', *The Hindu* (Meerat, 18 September 2014).
[88]'Moninder Pandhar gets bail, released from Dasna jail', *Business Standard* (Ghaziabad, 27 September 2014).

actions. It was almost as though this person, who is biologically a human being, could not feel the most human of all emotions, guilt and remorse for his actions, even when faced with the prospect of a hangman's noose.

Koli's motive to kill still remains open for speculation, and answers to these questions need to be found and investigated. Was it act of a deviant, mentally unstable individual or was it somehow influenced by society, which had driven Koli to commit such acts? Finding an answer to that question may help us fix whatever is wrong with the society we live in. If we do not address the larger problem, there could be another Koli, and more heinous acts could be committed.

There is another part of the story that is often overlooked. The residents of Nithari had been complaining to the local police for months prior to the discovery of the remains, about their missing children, and the police had been dismissing their complaints. It stated that these complaints did not warrant merit. In the aftermath of the discovery of these horrific murders, two beat police officers were removed from the police force for ignoring the complaints of the residents in the area. The victims were the children of poor migrant labourers who lived in slums. The failure of the police to register these complaints merely sheds light on the fact that in India, the children of the poor and the powerless, who are forgotten when alive, will be forgotten when dead as well.

The growing gap between India's rich and poor has resulted in the devaluation of human life. The life of a middle-class child seems to be worth more to the police than the life of a migrant labourer's child living in a rented hut. It takes such a heinous act for society to wake up and realize not only how vulnerable the children of the poor in India are, but also how the rich enjoy better facilities. It shows how painful it must be to be a poor person in this country and throws the world's largest democracy's egalitarian credentials into questionable spotlight.

SANJAY DUTT:
THE 'BHAI' OF BOLLYWOOD

'Insaaf na kanoon de sakta hai na police... agar koi insaaf de sakta hai... to ek insaan doosre insaan ko de sakta hai.[89]*'*

— Sanjay Dutt, as Ballu in *Khalnayak*

19 April 1993

When Sanjay Dutt arrived at the international airport in Mumbai from Mauritius, there were police waiting for him outside the airport. As soon as he emerged, he was arrested and whisked away. But this was not a surprise for Sanjay. His father, the iconic film actor Sunil Dutt, had himself called the Police Commissioner of Mumbai to inform him that his son would be returning to India on the night of 19 April 1993.

16 May 2013

Around 2.30 p.m., fifty-three-year-old Sanjay Dutt, accompanied by his wife Manyata, sister Priya Dutt, director Mahesh Bhatt and others, stepped out of his car into the narrow lane beside the sessions court premises in Mumbai. There was a huge crowd awaiting him—fans of the star who were shouting slogans, and

---

[89]Neither law nor police can deliver justice... only one person can deliver justice to another person.

members of the media who were desperately clicking pictures. After several minutes of persuasion, the crowd made way for Sanjay and he walked into the court premises. Sanjay Dutt, with his lawyer Rizwan Merchant by his side, walked into the court room and surrendered before the special TADA court. His prison sentence would start immediately.

A ROCKY JOURNEY

Sanjay Dutt is a man who polarizes opinions. In a country where film stars are worshipped, he undoubtedly has his share of followers. Several in the Hindi film industry consider him an innocent person who is still paying his dues for misdemeanours conducted in his youth. On the other hand, there are a substantial number who point at the evidence that has been racked up against him and ask, how, with the availability of such incriminatory evidence, can one even think of not sentencing Sanjay to the fullest extent possible under the law. Some believe that the media has portrayed him to be a victim of circumstances, while others go as far as to say that the courts have been lenient with him because of his celebrity status, in stark contrast to the verdicts handed out to his co-accused.

Born on 29 July 1959, Sanjay Dutt was the son of Sunil Dutt and Nargis, both beloved stars in the Hindi movie world through the 1940s to the 1960s. After his acting career, Sunil Dutt joined politics. He was elected for five terms to the parliament from the Mumbai north-west constituency. Nargis Dutt is considered one of the finest actresses of Hindi cinema. Though he was born to such illustrious parents, Sanjay has had a rocky journey over the years and most of this was his own doing.

He was a rebel without a cause. Unfortunately, because of

this misguided sense of rebellion, Sanjay developed a drug habit in his high school days. This only worsened after his mother's premature death in 1981 due to cancer, days before Sanjay's first movie was to be released. *Rocky*, produced and directed by Sunil Dutt to showcase his son, was a moderate hit. The songs and the general media hype around Nargis and Sunil Dutt's son propelled him into stardom—except that Sanjay was probably not ready for it yet. The death of his mother and the constant media attention worsened his drug addiction. In 1982, his father sent him to a rehabilitation centre in Texas, USA. He met his future wife, Richa Sharma, while in the US. After returning to India, Sanjay went back to acting in movies. He got good reviews for his performance in the movie *Naam*, which released in 1986. Soon after, in 1987, he married Richa. His life seemed to be coming back on track. With his tall muscular looks and long hair, he was a stark contrast to his contemporaries in the Hindi film industry. Some of his films from the late 1980s and early 1990s were big hits and he started acquiring a fan following. Movies like *Hathyar*, *Tejaa*, *Thanedaar*, *Sadak* and *Saajan* propelled him into superstardom. His acting in *Saajan* got him his first nomination for the Filmfare Best Actor Award. He was arrested by the police three weeks before the release of *Khalnayak*, the movie for which he won his second nomination for the Filmfare Best Actor Award, for his portrayal of a gangster with a heart of gold. It also proved to be one of the biggest hits of the time. However, Sanjay was fighting a different battle by then.

KHALNAYAK

After the demolition of the Babri Masjid on 6 December 1992, communal riots broke out in different parts of India, including in Mumbai. Violence escalated rapidly and the riots continued for over two months, from December 1992 to January 1993, which claimed the lives of hundreds of people, both Hindus and Muslims. Sunil Dutt helped many people, irrespective of their religion, during the riots. Such acts of benevolence during a frenzied riot earns one many enemies and the Dutt family received many threats.

Around the same time, some terrorists like Tiger Memon, Mohammed Kosa and Dawood Ibrahim formulated a conspiracy to carry out terrorist attacks in Mumbai in order to kill a larger number of people and further incite communal tension in India. Accordingly, shipments of arms and ammunitions were sent to Mumbai through the port, which were received by their henchmen.

On Friday, 12 March 1993, Mumbai was rocked by a series of twelve bomb blasts between 1.33 p.m. and 3.40 p.m., in which around 257 people were killed and another 713 injured. Property worth ₹27 crore was damaged.

While investigating the Mumbai blasts, the police got a lead about the smuggled arms and ammunitions. Further probing showed that Sanjay Dutt had been hiding some of the smuggled arms. Sanjay was not in India at that moment, as he was shooting for a movie in Mauritius. The police prepared to nab him as soon as he arrived back home. Sanjay was a well-known Bollywood actor, the son of a superstar and a well-known politician; the police did not have to worry about finding him. When the news that his son had been involved in smuggling arms reached his father, Sunil Dutt himself made a phone call to the Police Commissioner to inform him that Sanjay was expected to return from Mauritius on 19 April 1993.

On 18 April 1993, the police arrested one suspect, Mansoor

Ahmed, and on the next day, they arrested Sanjay soon after he landed at the international airport. On the same day, Sanjay made a statement to the police. He stated that a rifle, a pistol and the ammunitions were kept with Yusuf Nulwalla. He led the police force to Nulwalla's house in the Dongri Umarkhari neighbourhood. On reaching there, the police realized that Nulwalla had been detained at the Dongri police station for non-renewal of his arms license. Nulwalla was picked up and questioned by the CID and he quickly disclosed the name of Kersi Bapuji Adajania and led the police to his house. Adajania was also arrested by the police and interrogated. Adajania produced remnants of a burnt AK-56 rifle and led the police to Rusi Mulla, who led them to the house of Ajay Marwah. Marwah produced the pistol and its ammunition.

Based on statements of all these individuals and the evidence recovered, a criminal case (No. 21 of 1993) was registered against Sanjay Dutt, Nulwalla, Adajania, Rusi Mulla and Marwah, in pursuance to an existing case of CR No. 70 of 1993. Towards the end of April and the beginning of May, Sanjay, Nulwalla, Samir Hingora and Mansoor Ahmed confessed to the police, which provided them with further crucial information and evidence.

On 3 May 1993, Sanjay was sent to judicial custody. There was huge public interest regarding the case. Sanjay's father, Sunil Dutt, pleaded with his bitter rival, Balasaheb Thackeray, for the latter's support and Thackeray backed Sanjay in an unprecedented manner.

On 5 May 1993, Sanjay filed a writ petition before the Mumbai High Court and the court granted him interim bail, with the directive that the bail granted would continue till the filing of the charge sheet. After that, the court would again consider his bail application. On 4 November 1993, a consolidated charge sheet was filed against all accused persons.

In the meantime, though Sanjay was released on bail in May 1993 soon after his arrest, his bail application was subsequently dismissed by the designated court by its order dated 4 July 1993. Against this order, Sanjay filed a special leave petition before the Supreme Court. After hearing the matter, the case was referred to a constitutional bench of the Supreme Court in order to interpret of the provisions of TADA in relation to the case. Once the reference was decided by the constitutional bench, the matter was placed before the regular bench of the Supreme Court, which rejected the bail application.

On 9 November 1994, Sanjay Dutt filed for a detailed retraction of the statements he had made earlier. While discussing the motive behind the retraction, it is often assumed and debated that Sanjay extended cooperation on the assumption that he would only be charged under the Arms Act and therefore not have trouble receiving bail. But since the police were trying to connect him with the bomb blast and acts of terrorism, and were attempting to charge him under TADA, Sanjay and his coterie of advisors realized that their plan was going haywire. It may be a possibility that considering how the situation was unravelling, Sanjay decided that it was in his best interest to retract his earlier statements.

In June 1995, the central and the state governments set up a review committee to individually review the cases of every accused person in the bomb blasts, in order to determine whether the provisions of TADA were applicable against the accused and whether any of them could be entitled to bail. The public prosecutor decided that Sanjay was entitled to bail. The report was filed with the trial court on 9 August 1995. The CID submitted that they had no objection to granting bail to Sanjay, as well as eleven other accused.

In view of the report of the review committee, Sanjay renewed his application for bail before the designated court, which again rejected his application. On appeal against the order, the Supreme Court granted bail to Sanjay on 16 October 1995 till the completion of his trial.

The media hailed Sanjay's release from jail as his vindication. After he came out of jail, Sanjay resurrected his film career, acting in numerous films and establishing himself as one of the most bankable stars at the box office. He won his first Filmfare Award for Best Actor for his portrayal of a gangster in *Vaastav* in 1999. He received critical acclaim and award nominations for some of his other films as well. However, it was *Munnabhai MBBS* (2003) and *Lage Rago Munnabhai* (2006) that emerged to be his biggest hits and also picked up awards across the board.

However, all this while, the case against Sanjay and the other accused continued at the designated court. Finally, according to orders dated 28 November 2006 and 31 July 2007, the designated court convicted and sentenced Sanjay, Nulwalla and Adajania. Sanjay was sentenced to six years of rigorous imprisonment.

These orders were challenged by Sanjay Dutt and others before the Supreme Court, which the court finally dismissed on 21 March 2013.

VAASTAV

The extent of Sanjay's involvement in the crime was a moot question in the minds of the general public—Sanjay had bought the gun and ammunition in an attempt to protect his loved ones in an albeit reckless manner. The courts, however, had to decide whether it was simply naivety on his part or if he was involved with the gangsters and terrorists who had masterminded the Mumbai blasts. They could make a judgment on the truth only using the evidence available, which included the confessions of Sanjay and the other accused.

First, let us consider what Sanjay had stated in his confession to the police. According to him, he already had three licensed firearms, which he used for hunting. He had been introduced to Dawood Ibrahim and his brother Anees once in Dubai, during a film shoot by well-known actor and producer Firoz Khan. Sanjay admitted that he was well acquainted with Anees Ibrahim and had spent time with him. In January 1993, some of his producer friends, like Samir Hingora and Hanif Kandawala, told Sanjay that if he wished to acquire any firearm in order to ward off any threat to his family, they would be able to procure it for him. Sanjay did not show much interest in the beginning, but after much persuasion, he agreed. On 15 January 1993, Hingora and Kandawala came to meet Sanjay at his Pali Hill residence in the upmarket suburb of Bandra, along with another person called Abu Salem, and told him that they would provide him with the firearms the next day. Early next morning, the three came with a fourth person (Ibrahim Musa) whom Sanjay said he did not know. They had brought three AK-56s, about 250 rounds of ammunition and a few hand grenades with them. Sanjay told his friends that he only wanted one rifle and nothing else. They convinced Sanjay to keep the rifles and the ammunition on the condition that the extra weapons would be taken away later. After a few days, Hingora, Kandawala and Salem visited his place again and collected two of the rifles and some ammunitions. (Sanjay also said in his statement that while shooting in Dubai in September 1992, he had bought a 9-mm pistol from one

Kayuum, who was an associate of Dawood Ibrahim.) After purchasing the AK-56 rifle, Sanjay left for Mauritius for a film shoot. While there, he got to know that the police had arrested Hingora and Kandawala. Worried at the news, Sanjay then contacted Nullwala and had asked him to immediately remove the rifle and destroy it.

However, the confessions and statements made by the co-accused tell a different story.

Hingora said that he knew Anees Ibrahim and Chota Rajan through his business connections. Anees Ibrahim called him up sometime in mid-January 1993 and told him that Ibrahim Musa and Abu Salem, who were his men, had some weapons which needed to be delivered to Sanjay Dutt's residence. When Hingora accompanied the two men to Sanjay's place, the latter hugged Salem and asked them to bring the weapons next day. On 16 January 1993, nine AK-56 rifles were taken to Sanjay's home, of which he was given three along with some ammunition. Sanjay apparently also asked for some hand grenades, which were also left with him.

Mansoor Ahmed revealed in his confession that Abu Salem and he had once taken a bagful of weapons to an old lady called Zaibunisa Kazi at 22 Mount Mary, Vidhyanchal Apartments. On another occasion, both of them had received a blue rexin bag and a carton from Sanjay at his residence, which they delivered to Zaibunisa Kazi for safekeeping. Furthermore, he said that she had been informed that the material would be used for orchestrating bomb blasts.

The prosecution laid emphasis on the confession made by Sanjay Dutt before the police after his arrest. Normally in India, confessions made before the police are inadmissible in a court of law. However, since Sanjay was charged under TADA, a particular provision of that law stated that a confession made by a person before a police officer no lower in rank than a superintendent of police and recorded by the police in writing or on any mechanical device, shall be admissible in the trial of such a person or co-accused, abettor or conspirator for an offence under TADA, provided that the co-accused, abettor or conspirator is charged and tried in the same case together with the accused. The prosecution contended that even though Sanjay retracted his confessions subsequently, a voluntary and free confession, even if later retracted, can be relied upon. In this case, the retraction happened months later, and therefore, was an afterthought.

It was, however, contended by the advocates that the court cannot rely on his confession. It was argued that if the provision led to a situation where a confession to the police becomes admissible irrespective of the fate of the TADA charge, then it would lead to invidious discrimination between the accused who were charged but subsequently acquitted under TADA along with other offences, and those who were accused only of non-TADA offences. It was further argued that mere possession of a weapon is not an offence under TADA. Section 5 merely raises a presumption that a person who is in possession of unauthorized arms or ammunition of a specified variety, would be liable for punishment under TADA. However, in this case, it could not be proved that Sanjay was going to utilize the arms and ammunition for the blasts.

Referring to the confession, his advocates contended that assuming that all the statements given by him were correct (even though the confession was retracted later), it still does not prove his involvement in the bomb blast conspiracy. They argued that if Sanjay had purchased weapons illegally, without having obtained a license, he should be convicted under the Arms Act and not TADA, like the other accused. It was further advanced that Sanjay had obtained the weapons when the riots were going on in Mumbai, much before the blasts took place. They contended that he had been merely trying to safeguard his family. It was argued that from the evidence available, it is not possible to assume that Sanjay was connected to the blasts or that he acquired weapons for that purpose.

On the basis of the available evidence and the arguments and counter-arguments put forward by the advocates of both sides, Justice Sathasivam convicted Sanjay Dutt for offences punishable under Sections 3 and 7 read with Sections 25(1-A), (1-B)(a) of the Arms Act, 1959. However, he was pronounced not guilty for all the other offences for which he had been charged, including those under TADA. Sanjay was sentenced to rigorous imprisonment for five years by the Supreme Court, reducing the initial sentence from six, as had been passed by the TADA court. When Sanjay's advocates requested the court to release him on probation on the basis of his past behaviour, the court refused to do so.

Considering that he had already spent eighteen months in jail at the time of the verdict, Sanjay would have to serve another three years and six months in jail.

AGNEEPATH

When the Supreme Court confirmed the verdict and Sanjay decided to accept it without appealing the judgment, it brought an end to a two-decade-old saga, but it did not bury all the questions around the trial. While there were a group of people—several from the film industry and others including politicians and ex-judges—who advocated leniency to be shown to Sanjay, there was an equally vocal counter movement which insisted that the investigating agencies and the prosecution were handling Sanjay with kid gloves unnecessarily.

The arguments which were put forth to seek Sanjay's pardon were that he had been young and immature when the incident took place, that he was a family man and has kids to support, that he has acted in movies which have promoted non-violence and harmony, so on and so forth. Needless to say, such arguments are juvenile and irrelevant and the propagators gained nothing but some media attention.

However, there are some bigger issues which have posed some unanswered questions:

- In 1993, why did the police not search Sanjay's house when they first obtained information about his involvement in a crime? Instead, the news had been leaked to newspapers, after which Sanjay instructed Nulwalla to destroy the evidence.

- To what extent was Sanjay involved with Anees Ibrahim? There was some information that showed that phone calls had been made from Sanjay's home to Anees Ibrahim in Dubai. But no further information seems to be available on this and there was no mention of it in the submission of the prosecution in court.

- There is unconfirmed news that Sanjay was in touch with members of Dawood Ibrahim's gang even when he was out on bail. It is also believed that the Mumbai police recorded a telephonic conversation between Sanjay and Chota Shakeel. However, neither did the police take any action on basis of such alleged conversations, nor was this brought up by the prosecution to seek the cancellation of Sanjay's bail.

Now that the proceedings are over and wrapped up, these questions will never be answered.

Sanjay Dutt's fans and supporters are, however, in no mood to find fault with the prosecution. They were distraught that their beloved 'Sanju baba' was put behind bars, but they were also relieved because they knew that it could have been for a much longer duration had Sanjay been convicted of the other offences of which he had been accused.

Sanjay Dutt himself seems to have come to terms with the reality of the situation. Whatever be the offences that he had committed, ever since he was released on bail in 1995, he has gradually emerged as a respectable and responsible actor in the Hindi movie industry. The manner in which he had worked hard to shoot for the films that he had signed on before surrendering to the authorities speaks of his professionalism. This has earned him respect and gratitude amongst his colleagues in the industry.

AUTHORS' NOTE

It is true that Sanjay has suffered over the years, but one should not forget that it was with due reason. As much as he suffered due to the court cases, he also used it to his advantage to construct the image of a lovable gangster—an image that he and his producers have exploited in innumerable films. At the same time, we cannot forget that he has taken blows to his chin and has stood up to face reality. He cooperated with the police from the very beginning and has accepted the sentence with dignity. The path Sanjay had trodden in his youth had been a crooked one, one that had taken him to prison. But if the main objective of punishment is reformation, it would probably be right to say that in this case, it was a success. With anyone else, a sentence such as this would probably have meant the end of their career. But with Sanjay Dutt, producers and fans waited for him to emerge from prison, just like he had done in so many of his movies.

THE PARLIAMENT ATTACK CASE

'This was not just an attack on the building, it was a warning to the entire nation. We accept the challenge.'

—Atal Bihari Vajpayee

THE PARLIAMENT ATTACK of 13 December 2001 was an event that shook the nation's sense of security. Until that day, the Sansad Bhavan, which accommodates both houses of the parliament, was considered the most secure place in the country. The complex symbolized what many believe is the greatest achievement of modern India—a vibrant, functional democracy. On that fateful day, five men armed with assault rifles, plastic explosives and hand grenades entered the grounds of the Sansad Bhavan in a white Ambassador and staged what the then home minister, L.K. Advani described as a Fedayeen attack. It was an attack on the heart of Indian ethos, on its most secular institution and the repository of a nation's faith.

The US state department officially stated that the objective of the attack was to shake the foundations of Indian democracy. The attackers killed seven people and left eighteen injured. On 15 December 2001, the Delhi police arrested Afzal Guru, an alleged member of the Jaish-e-Mohammad. It was alleged that Afzal Guru had conspired and sheltered the terrorists who had perpetrated such an audacious and unseemly attack on the parliament. His arrest was followed by arrests of S.A.R. Gilani, Afsan Guru and Shaukat Hussein.

SPECIAL COURT TRIAL

The evidentiary standard established by law requires an offence to be proven beyond reasonable doubt to convict a person. That is, the evidence must not leave any gap for any reasonable doubt as to a person's innocence.

The police recovered three cell phones and six SIM cards from the bodies of the dead militants. The evidence linking the accused persons to the attack on the parliament was the telephone records of the deceased terrorists—all the six SIM cards indicated that they had communicated with Afzal Guru on his mobile phone. The records also indicated that there had been communication with Shaukat Hussein on his cell phone. He, however, denied having possessed the phone number in question. Shaukat Hussein and Afzal Guru were relatives; S.A.R. Gilani was acquainted with both, as he had performed the marriage of Shaukat Hussein with Afsan Guru.

On 14 December 2001, in the course of surveillance, the Delhi police picked up a conversation in Kashmiri, in which S.A.R. Gilani had allegedly supported the attack on the parliament. Phone records also indicated that Shaukat Hussein and his wife Afsan Guru had spoken about the parliament attack in a positive light.

The defence's case in the special court rested on the procedural lapses during the investigation. The defence raised questions about whether the sanction for trial under the

Prevention of Terrorism Act, 2002 (POTA)[90] and the Explosive Substances Act had been obtained in accordance with the respective Acts. The defence also questioned the veracity and credibility of the evidence presented by the prosecution, and it alleged that the case was a conspiracy against the accused. The defence also raised doubts about the admissibility of telephonic interceptions as evidence under the POTA.

In the judgment, the judge accepted the prosecution's arguments, and in case of inconsistencies, used reasonable explanations to ensure that the prosecution's case stood, despite there having been no direct evidence to indicate a link between the four accused persons and the five deceased militants. The evidence connecting the alleged conspiracy and the deceased militants was only circumstantial in nature. Despite there being no direct evidence, three of the accused were convicted in this case, while Afsan Guru was acquitted.

What is of particular interest in this case is that Afzal Guru was convicted and sentenced to death on the basis of a confession recorded by a police officer in the absence of any other persons. His was in writing and was signed by him.

THE DELHI HIGH COURT APPEAL

The Delhi High Court, in its decision,[91] extensively discussed the

---

[90]The POTA was enacted to make provisions for the prevention of, and for dealing with, terrorist activities that were carried on in India. However, as there were allegations of POTA being grossly misused for political purposed, on 7 October 2004, the union cabinet under the UPA government approved the repeal of POTA.

[91]*State vs. Mohd Afzal and Ors.* 107(2003) DLT 385.

evidence used to convict the three accused, and also discussed the standards of evidence required to convict a person of an offence. It examined the transcripts of the telephone conversation used to convict S.A.R. Gilani and found that they did not prove beyond a reasonable doubt that S.A.R. Gilani was a conspirator in the offence.

Gilani had admitted that he sympathized with the militant organization in question, however, he denied having been a member of it. The conversation under consideration did not indicate any reference to the attack and so the Delhi High Court acquitted S.A.R. Gilani. It is pertinent to note that the acquittal created a significant impact on the prosecution's case, as it had maintained that S.A.R. Gilani was the mastermind behind the parliament attack.

During the appeal, Afzal Guru's counsel claimed that Guru had been inadequately represented in the special court trial. The right to a fair trial is a founding cornerstone of any democracy. Under the Legal Services Authority Act, 1987, every person who is an indigent has the right to free legal aid. The objective of the legislation is to provide free and competent legal aid to the weaker sections of society. In this case, the competence of the legal aid provided in the special court trial was questioned during the appeal before the Delhi High Court. The right to legal aid is derived from the principle of natural justice, which requires all parties in a matter to be heard. If the person is unable to access appropriate counsel, or if the counsel in question is unable to perform his duty properly due to any kind of pressure, one could go so far as to say that it denies the person the opportunity to a fair trial.

The Delhi High Court held that as Afzal Guru had not expressed a need to change counsel during the course of the trial, the claim of inadequate representation would not stand. The court also held that the question of inadequacy was a subjective one, and with no mechanical standard to determine it, it could not be used as grounds for retrial. However, human rights organizations were outraged by the inadequacy of representation given to Afzal Guru. The Peoples Union for Civil Liberties filed an appeal before the Delhi High Court.

The evidence examined also included the deposition of one Subhash Chand Malhotra, who was the landlord of a house rented by Afzal Guru. In the deposition, Malhotra claimed that on the day of the attack, he had seen Afzal Guru and Shaukat Hussein leave the premises with four other persons in a white Ambassador. The deposition also included his statement verifying the police search and seizure on 16 December 2001. He stated that the police had found twenty jars containing sulphur. While being cross-examined about the veracity of this claim, he admitted that he was unaware of the jars' contents. He also revealed that the deposition, which was in English, had been written by the police and had been read to him, after which he signed it. He admitted that he only knew how to read and write in Hindi.

The deposition was accepted as evidence and was used to convict Afzal Guru and Shaukat Hussein. However, one could argue that the deposition does not meet evidentiary standards since it could be contended that the content of the deposition was completely controlled by the police and may have been recorded with prior prejudice against Afzal Guru and Shaukat Hussein. The opinion of a common man, such as the one making the deposition, may have also been coloured by the media portrayal of Afzal Guru's guilt. One cannot ignore the possible influence and impact this would have had on the mind of the deponent.

THE SUPREME COURT DECISION

Following the appeal,[92] the Supreme Court reduced Shaukat Hussein's sentence to rigorous imprisonment for a period of ten years under S. 123 of the IPC. The reduction of the sentence was a result of the lack of direct evidence linking Shaukat Hussein to the conspiracy. The Supreme Court stated that mere suspicion could not be used as grounds for proof of guilt. The court used circumstantial evidence to convict Shaukat Hussein of concealing with intent to wage war, as the evidence indicated that he was seen in constant contact with Afzal Guru and eyewitness accounts suggested that Shaukat Hussein would regularly visit Afzal Guru, and was also seen with him prior to the attack.

The Supreme Court, however, dismissed Afzal Guru's appeal. The court upheld the death sentence awarded by the special court.

MERCY PETITION AND HANGING

Afzal Guru's wife, Tabasum Guru, filed a mercy petition before the former president, A.P.J. Abdul Kalam, on 3 October 2003. The mercy petition was followed by a plea before the Supreme Court to review the death sentence. The petition was dismissed for lack of merit.

On 3 February 2013, President Pranab Mukherjee rejected

---

[92] *State (NCT of Delhi) vs. Navjot Sandhu @ Afsan Guru and Ors*, 2005(11) SCC 600.

the mercy petition. This was the second such mercy petition to be rejected by President Mukherjee. The news of the rejection was sent to Afzal Guru's family by registered post. On 9 February 2013, Afzal Guru was hung until dead at the Tihar Jail complex in Delhi. The news of the hanging became public only after the fact.

The hanging led to protests by human rights organizations in Delhi as well as Jammu and Kashmir. The Jammu and Kashmir Chief Minister, Omar Abdullah, was reported to have said, 'One of the biggest tragedies of the execution was the further alienation of Kashmiris.'[93] Curfew was enforced in Afzal Guru's hometown, Sopore, in northern Jammu and Kashmir, in order to maintain law and order on the day of the hanging. The curfew, however, was not sufficient, and additional police and paramilitary forces were required to be brought in.[94]

AUTHORS' NOTE

The international media went on to call the trial a 'trial by the media'. Some international news networks called the hanging of Afzal Guru a 'selective hanging,'[95] as Afzal Guru was hanged before other inmates on death row, such as those convicted for the assassination of former Prime Minister Rajeev Gandhi, or the person found guilty for the assassination of the Punjab Chief Minister, Beant Singh.

---

[93]'Why the rush to execute one? Hang Rajiv, Beant killers too: Omar', *Times of India* (Srinagar/New Delhi, 11 February 2013).

[94]Neha Thirani Bagri, 'Amid Protests, India Executes Man in '01 Parliament Attack,' *The New York Times* (Mumbai, 9 February 2013).

[95]Sudha G Tilak, 'Indian Hanging Raises Doubts Over Timing,' *Al Jazeera* (India, 13 February 2013).

The Indian media was considered responsible for instigating the civil society to demand death which, in turn, put additional pressure on the state. The media's aggressive call for the hanging originated with the 26/11 attacks, where there was a call for the implementation of the death penalty for Kasab in that case.

The influence of the media was also clear when various counsels appointed for Afzal Guru were apparently pressurized socially and even politically to withdraw themselves from the case. It is important to keep in mind that under the Advocates Act, 1961, a lawyer may only refuse a brief on two grounds—either inadequacy of fees or lack of expertise in the subject matter. In the case at hand, the question of inadequacy of fees or the lack of expertise was not appropriate grounds for the withdrawal as the counsels were appointed by the state legal services authority. The pressure of the media may have restricted a person's right to a fair trial, which he is entitled to. Though the Delhi High Court had rejected the contention, the doubt lingered in the minds of many people, even after Afzal Guru was hanged.

BIBLIOGRAPHY

JUDICIAL DECISIONS

1. *Bodh Raj vs. State of Jammu & Kashmir* [AIR 2002 SC 3164].
2. *Central Bureau Of Investigation vs. V.C. Shukla & Ors*, [(1998) 3 SCC 410].
3. *Charles Sobhraj vs. State*, [(1996) CriLJ 3354].
4. *Delhi Development Authority vs. Skipper Construction Pvt. Ltd. and Another* [1996 SCC [1] 272].
5. *Dhananjay Chatterjee Alias Dhana vs. State Of W.B.* [1994 (1) ALT Cri 388].
6. *Jennison vs. Baker*, [(1972) 1 All England Reporter 997].
7. *Ketan Parkeh vs. Securities Exchange Board of India*, [Securities Appellate Tribunal judgment dated 14 July 2006].
8. *Mohammed Ajmal Mohammed Amir Kasab vs. State of Maharashtra* [(2012) 8 S.C.R 295].
9. *P.V. Narasimha Rao vs. State* [AIR 1998 SC 2120].
10. *R. Venkatakrishnan vs. Central Bureau of Investigation* [2009 (8) TMI 695].
11. *Sanjay Dutt vs. State of Maharashtra* [Supreme Court judgment dated 21 March 2013].
12. *Santosh Kumar Singh vs. State (Through CBI)* [(2010) 9 SCC 747].
13. *Shankar vs. State of Tamil Nadu* [1994 SCC (4) 478].
14. *Shatrughan Chauhan & Anr vs. Union of India & Ors.* [(2014) 3 SCC 1].

15. *Sidhartha Vashisht alias Manu Sharma vs. State* (Nct Of Delhi) [(2010) 6 SCC 1].
16. *State (NCT of Delhi) vs. Navjot Sandhu and Afsan Guru and Ors* [2005(11) SCC 600].
17. *State (Through CBI) vs. Santosh Kumar Singh* [2007 CriLJ 964].
18. *State of Tamil Nadu through Superintendent of Police, CBI/SIT vs. Nalini & Ors.* [(1999) 5 SCC 253].
19. *State of Uttar Pradesh vs. Charles Sobhraj* [AIR 1996 SC 3473].
20. *State vs. Mohd Afzal and Ors.* [107(2003) DLT 385].
21. *State vs. Sushil Sharma* [2007 CriLJ 4008].
22. *Sudhir Shantilal Mehta vs. C.B.I,* [(2009) INSC 1421].
23. *Sunil Batra vs. Delhi administration & Ors.* [AIR 1978 SC 1675].
24. *Surendra Koli vs. State of Uttar Pradesh* [(2011) 4 SCC 80].
25. *Sushil Sharma vs. State (NCT) Of Delhi,* [(2014) 4 SCC 317].
26. *The Chairman, Railway Board & Ors vs. Mrs Chandrima Das & Ors* [AIR 2000 SC 988].
27. *Vikas Yadav vs. State of Uttar Pradesh* [High Court of Delhi judgment dated 7 August 2009].
28. *Vishaka & Ors vs. State of Rajasthan & Ors,* [JT 1997 (7) SC 384].
29. *Vishal Yadav vs. State of Uttar Pradesh* [High Court of Delhi judgment dated 7 August 2009].
30. *Zahria Habibullah Sheik vs. State of Gujarat* [AIR 2006 SC 1367].

BOOKS AND ARCHIVAL SOURCES

1. Ankur Chawal, *14 Hours: An Insider's Account of the 26/11 Taj Attack*, Rupa & Co., 2012.
2. Arun Kumar, *Black Economy in India*, Penguin, 2002.
3. Cathy Scott-Clark, *The Siege—The Attack on the Taj* by Adrian Levy, Penguin, 2013.
4. Debashis Basu, Sucheta Dalal. *The Scam: From Harshad Metha to Ketan Parekh*, KenSource Information Services, 2007.
5. *Joint Committee on Stock Market Scam and Matters Relating Thereto* (Thirteenth Lok Sabha) (Volume I—Report).
6. N. Vittal, *Ending Corruption?—How to Clean Up India*, Penguin, 2012.
7. Raymond W. Baker, *Capitalism's Achilles Heel: Dirty Money and how to renew the Free Market System*, John Wiley and Sons Inc., 2005.
8. Richard Neville & Julie Clarke, *The Life and Crimes of Charles Sobhraj*, PAN, 1980.
9. Rommel Rodrigues, *Kasab: The Face of 26/11*, Penguin, 2010.
10. Thomas Thompson, Serpentine, Carrol & Graf Publishers Inc. New York, 2000.
11. Vir Sanghvi, *26/11: The Attack on Mumbai*, Penguin, 2009.

NEWS PAPERS AND JOURNALS

1. *The Deccan Herald*
2. *The Hindu*
3. *Hindustan Times*
4. *The Indian Express*

5. *The Statesman*
6. *The Telegraph*

NEWS WEBSITES

1. *Al Jazeera,* http://www.aljazeera.com/
2. *BBC World News,* http://www.bbc.com/news/world/
3. *IBN Live,* http://ibnlive.in.com/
4. *Indolink,* http://www.indolink.com/
5. *Rediff News,* http://www.rediff.com/news
6. *The New York Times,* http://www.nytimes.com/
7. *The Independent,* http://www.independent.co.uk/
8. *India Today,* http://indiatoday.intoday.in/
9. *The Guardian,* http://www.theguardian.com/uk
10. *Zee News,* http://zeenews.india.com/
11. *NDTV,* http://www.ndtv.com/
12. *The Times,* http://www.thetimes.co.uk/tto/news/

ACKNOWLEDGEMENTS

The authors acknowledge the contribution and help of the following people without whom the book would not have been a possibility:

Mr R.K. Mehra of Rupa & Co., who suggested the idea of this book and the editorial team at Rupa & Co. for their patience and hard work that was instrumental in making this book a reality.

Mr Deepto Roy of PXV Law Partners, for his encouragement and many ideas on the name.

Mr Ajay Kumar, Mr Vishal Srinivas, Ms Rukmini Das, Ms Sneha Agnihotri, Ms Namritha Joseph, Shreya Asopa and Tanmayee Sahoo for their excellent research and hard work.